From a Stretcher Handle: The World War I Journal & Poems of Pte. Frank Walker

From a Stretcher Handle:
The
World War I Journal & Poems
of
Pte. Frank Walker

Edited by
Mary F. Gaudet

Theresa
With all best
wishes Mary F. Gaudet

Institute of Island Studies
Charlottetown
2000

*Editing:*Edward MacDonald, Laurie Brinklow
Design: UPEI Graphics
Printing: Williams & Crue Ltd., Summerside, PEI

The Institute of Island Studies gratefully acknowledges the financial support of the Prince Edward Island Millennium Committee.

Canadian Cataloguing in Publication Data
Walker, Frank, b. 1893
    From a stretcher handle
    ISBN 0-919013-40-6
1. Walker, Frank, b. 1893 — Diaries.   2. World War, 1914–1918 — Poetry.
    3. World
War, 1914–1918 — Personal narratives, Canadian. I. Gaudet, Mary. F., 1928–
II. University of Prince Edward Island. Institute of Island Studies.
    III. Title.

PS8545.A468F76 2000   C811'52   C00-95013-4
PR9199.3.W3418F76 2000

Institute of Island Studies Publishing Committee
John Cousins (Chair)
Harry Baglole
Laurie Brinklow
John Crossley
Donna Giberson
Allan Hammond
Michael Hennessey
Catherine Innes-Parker
Deirdre Kessler
Edward MacDonald
Ian MacQuarrie

Institute of Island Studies
University of Prince Edward Island
Charlottetown, PE Canada C1A 4P3
tel: (902)566-0956
fax: (902)566-0756
e-mail: iis@upei.ca
website: www.islandstudies.com

Dedicated
to all veterans and victims
of war

The Guide

"Yea! Though I walk through the Valley
of the shadow of Death, I will fear no
Evil, for Thou art with me…"

Just when the sun sinks behind the sombre drooping
        trees,
Ere yet the sentry-stars their customed watch have
        ta'en;
With weary, patient step, amid the guns' loud
        blasphemies,
Christ leads the stretcher-squads over the Fields of Pain.

Contents

Acknowledgements

In 1997 I began to edit and research my father's War Journal for publication. For over a year and a half it was my privilege to draw upon the wisdom, knowledge, experience, and generosity of a number of individuals who, in turn, gave freely of their time and expertise.

I am deeply indebted to my mentor, Dr. David Beatty, long-time Associate Professor of History and now Professor Emeritus, Mount Allison University, Sackville, New Brunswick, and author of many articles and two books on Canada and World War I. His books are cited in my Bibliography. Dr. Beatty's personal support, recommendations of related texts and conventions, his reading of the early drafts of the Introduction and Epilogue, and help with revisions were critical to me throughout the preparation of the manuscript for publication.

Special thanks to Dr. Vaughn Alward, Education Consultant in Sackville, whom I met in the summer of 1997 and who was responsible for the initial contact between Dr. Beatty and myself; Rev. Father Wendell MacIntyre, author and retired English professor, University of Prince Edward Island, who gave helpful direction in the early stages of this project; Susan Gallant, Secretary, Faculty Association, University of Prince Edward Island, whose word processing skills and congenial personality carried us through multiple revisions; and Barbara Morgan, photographer, who made negatives from the original photos and reproduced the required size without sacrificing the quality.

My gratitude to others who assisted me in research: Donna Porter, Directorate of History and Heritage, Department of National Defence, Ottawa, and former student of Dr. Beatty; Sergeant Ron Gaudet (our son), Communications Security Establishment, Ottawa, who arranged a meeting for me with Ms. Porter in September 1997; Mike Acker and David Panton, Commemorations, Department of Veterans Affairs Canada, Charlottetown, for their personal support and helpful suggestions; Joyce Gaudet, Librarian, Department of Veterans Affairs Canada; the late Martin Dorrell, Journalism Instructor, Holland College; Dr. Peter Liddle, Leeds University, Leeds, UK; and Betty Jeffrey and Sharon Flynn, Reference Librarians, Robertson Library, UPEI, Charlottetown.

Sincere appreciation to the Institute of Island Studies, University of Prince Edward Island, for publishing the manuscript, including Director Harry Baglole; Publishing Co-ordinator Laurie Brinklow, for her expertise and attention to detail; former Institute Director of Research and now Associate Professor of History at UPEI, Dr. Ed MacDonald, who edited the Introduction and Epilogue; to historian Boyde Beck of the PEI Museum and Heritage Foundation; Greg Gallant, PEI Regiment Museum, for unearthing the postcard that graces the book's cover; and to all relatives and friends who contributed their interest and encouragement.

My gratitude to my husband Jim, for his love and patience in photo-copying reams of print; our daughters Marlene, Lynn, Valerie, Dayna, and Jan, and our son Ron, for their valuable input.

Remembering my brother George, a Korean War veteran who died in 1993. Special thanks to my brother John Walker and sisters Millie Trainor and Pat Richard for their encouragement and support for the publication of Dad's historic legacy.

To my father:
> O then the bliss of blisses, to be freed
> From all the wants by which the world is driven
> With liberty and endless time to read
> The libraries of Heaven!
>
> —Author unknown

Mary F. Gaudet

"You Have No Idea..."
Stretcher Bearers in the Great War

Boyde Beck

"If I had thousands of Victoria Crosses to distribute,
all would go to stretcher-bearers."
— *General William Birdwood, Commander, 5th Army, 1918*

Between 1914 and 1918, five empires and numerous nations waged what was arguably the bloodiest war in human history. Certainly no other battlefield in the history of warfare was as lethal as the Great War's Western Front. Britain and its Empire threw six million men and women into the battle for Belgium and France. Close to three million were wounded. Of these, nine hundred thousand died. "Medical services were not just there to serve a few unfortunates," observes historian John Ellis. "[They] were as integral a part of the front line soldier's life as ration parties or his own officers."

The British Army devoted fifteen per cent of its fighting strength to the swift evacuation and treatment of its wounded. It was considered vital to morale. Removing injured soldiers quickly from the battlefield was proof to those left in the line that they would be well looked after if their turn came. It also improved the Army's chances of being able to use the soldier again once he was healed. Many thousands of men were returned to combat after suffering wounds that in previous wars would have ended, if not their lives, then at least their usefulness as soldiers.

Modeled entirely on its British Army counterpart, The Royal Canadian Army Medical Corps (RCAMC) was created in 1906. In 1914 the Corps had 127 officers and personnel. By the end of 1918 it had over 15,500 in uniform. They did very well, considering how little the war they fought was like the one they'd been planning for. Prior to the Great War, disease, not shells or bullets, had been the main cause of death in warfare. Britain's experience in South Africa between 1899 and 1902 reinforced this idea, and, when its Royal Army Medical Corps was reorganized after that war, great emphasis was placed on maintaining hygiene and treating diseases before they could spread. In this the Medical Corps in the Great War performed beyond expectation. Even though its troops lived and fought in conditions that tested the strongest of constitutions, only seven per cent of the deaths in the Canadian Expeditionary Force were attributed to disease. The RCAMC treated 400,000 reported cases of illness and lost only 3,800 — a cure rate of over ninety-nine per cent.

A much more severe test of the Medical Services came in the treatment of wounds. From the politicians who declared the war, through the Generals who supervised it, to the men who fought it, the Great War surprised everyone with how dangerous combat had become. Advanced weaponry, combined with the sheer size of the armies involved, created the biggest, deadliest battlefield in history. Artillery caused the most suffering; seventy per cent of wounds were caused by shrapnel and shell fragments. Shrapnel was usually in the form of small lead pellets, though, by the end of the war, resource-starved Germany was packing its shrapnel rounds with a variety of scrap metal. Shrapnel wounds were invariably multiple, demanding hours of surgery to clean up. Shell fragments caused more hideous wounds, often weighing several pounds and hitting their victims like an old-fashioned cannon ball — with jagged edges. These wounds were disfiguring, but if they didn't kill instantly they could be treated. Appearances could be deceiving, historian Robin Keirstead writes: "The members of the Medical Corps quickly learned that the size of a wound and amount of bleeding were not always true indicators of the seriousness of the injury. Some of the most innocent-looking wounds proved to be the most serious, while some of the most ghastly turned out to have caused little real damage."

Bullets accounted for most of the other thirty per cent of wounds. The lucky ones were hit by single rifle rounds. Small-calibre, high-velocity bullets made small, surprisingly easy-to-treat wounds, at least if they didn't hit bone, a major blood vessel, or a vital organ. But most bullet wounds were caused by machine guns. These were usually fired from dug-in positions, and it was the practice for machine gunners to aim low, for the legs, causing the wounded man to fall into the stream of bullets. "If he is hit at all," wrote stretcher bearer Frederick Pottle, "he is likely to be riddled." Surprisingly, two of the Great War's more well-known weapons — the bayonet and the gas shell — accounted for a vanishingly small percentage of its casualties. For all the emphasis armies put on training recruits to wield their bayonets, less than one per cent of the wounds treated during the war were from this cause. Gas proved to be more a psychological than a deadly weapon, accounting for less than two per cent of the casualties in the CEF.

The variety and severity of the wounds being treated on a given day at one of the Medical Corps' forward positions was not a sight for the faint-hearted. "It is a good thing not to be too squeamish," wrote one observer in 1916. "The smell of septic limbs and heads is enough to bowl one over. As usual, a good many deaths, one had the back of his head off, another from the nose down completely gone. But it is the multiple wounds that appear worst, men almost in pieces, the number intensifies the horror, we get so few slight cases." Despite this, the wounded had a surprisingly good survival rate. According to its official history, RCAMC treated 150,000 wounded in the Great War, losing 17,000. In other words, if you were wounded in combat and didn't die immediately, the Medical Corps had a close to ninety per cent chance of saving your life.

The first stage of treatment was often the wounded man himself. Every British soldier kept within his tunic a "First Field Dressing"—a sterile gauze pad attached to several feet of sterile bandage and a phial of iodine, all wrapped neatly in a waterproof bundle about the size of a modern soft drink can. The dressing could be opened with one hand, if necessary; it could stanch the flow of blood from a simple wound and, more importantly, keep it clean.

The next step was getting noticed. Men hit in their own trenches could be quickly attended to, but those wounded during an assault were in graver danger. Sometimes, usually after a major battle, sectors on both sides would observe informal truces to let stretcher parties search the battlefield for their wounded. But these occasions were rare, especially as the war wore on. If the wounded man couldn't make his way back to his own lines on his own or with the help of comrades, his future was bleak. There were stories of miraculous recoveries of wounded men stranded two, three, or more days in some shell hole. Such stories were miraculous because they were so rare. Seventy per cent of the Canadians who died in battle never got the chance to receive medical assistance. Many of these no doubt died of relatively treatable wounds.

Once back on their own side of the battlefront, the wounded were taken to a Regimental Aid Post: one per battalion or four per regiment. Here the casualties were assessed and given whatever treatment was needed to stabilize them. Those with mild wounds—"Blighties" in the British Army slang, "Blessé" in the French—were sent back on their own, if they were able to walk, or waited for the more seriously wounded to be evacuated before being stretchered out. The more serious cases sometimes caused the Regimental Medical Officer to ask some hard questions of himself. "Will the man die if he's moved any further?" "Can his condition be stabilized enough to allow him to be moved?" "How much time will this take?" And the hardest question of all: "Is there another man here who might survive if I treat him, but die if I don't because I'm working on this man, who will probably die no matter what I do?" Those who were deemed able to survive the trip to further treatment were stabilized and made ready for their journey. Those deemed not were made as comfortable as possible until they died.

The next stage was the trip down the line to an Advanced Dressing Station. The Regimental Aid Posts were essentially part of the front line, positioned a few hundred yards, at most, from the forward trench system. The Dressing Stations were about a mile to the rear, still within range of most artillery and machine gun fire, but far enough back to allow more thorough treatment. A patient's stay here was as brief as possible. After further assessment and possibly a fresh set of bandages, he was loaded onto a horse or motor ambulance for the trip back to the Casualty Clearing Station.

Providing medical services in combat was a fine balancing act. Trained medical officers or combat surgeons were precious personnel, far too valuable to be stationed too near the front lines. Yet, if they were too far back, an unacceptable number of wounded would die before getting a chance to be treated. Early Medical Corps doctrine dictated that the Casualty Clearing Stations simply do what their name implied: clear the casualties from the battlefield to the Stationary, General, and Base hospitals that were set up safely in the rear. But, as the war went on, more treatment was done in the forward areas. By 1916 the Casualty Clearing Station combined the atmosphere of the forward aid posts with the services of a fairly sophisticated hospital. This is where most of the emergency surgery was done; internal wounds were sutured and stabilized, limbs too badly shattered to be repaired were amputated. In the aftermath of a major battle, the CCS would look like something from a nightmare: ground covered with stretchers, walking wounded waiting patiently for their turn, heaps of rags that turn out to be piles of amputated limbs, and the tumult of eighty-five harried surgeons and orderlies dealing with hundreds of badly injured soldiers. But there was order in the chaos, and the treatment received here often decided whether the casualty would live or die.

After the journey to Casualty Clearing Station, the trip to the Stationary Hospital must have seemed leisurely. In general, a wounded soldier who survived until reaching one of the hospitals in the rear was probably going to survive his wound. From here, on recovery, he would be returned to active service if still able to serve. From here, if the wound required rehabilitation or discharge from service, he would be sent home.

Perhaps the most critical segment of a wounded man's journey was the trip from the Regimental Aid Post to the Forward Dressing Station. There was no way to get horse or motor transport this far forward. The wounded had to be carried out by hand. This was the job of the Field Ambulances. Each division was assigned three Field Ambulances, each manned by nine officers and 238 "other ranks." Each Ambulance in turn was divided into a Tent Company and a Bearer Company. The Tent Company was responsible for treating the wounded once they arrived. The Bearer Company was responsible for getting them there. The tools of the stretcher bearer's trade were not complicated: a folding canvas-and-wood stretcher, a shoulder strap to help shift some of the weight of a full stretcher onto the back muscles, and a white arm band with "SB" printed in large black letters. The skills demanded were mainly physical: the ability to carry a heavy weight in a steady manner over a long distance. However, many also became expert in dressing and re-bandaging wounds, freeing front line Medical Officers for other tasks. They were excused from most routine chores—"fatigues"—when off duty, and the sight of a bearer company loafing in the sun was always good for a chorus of catcalls, or worse, from any regular infantrymen who happened to be passing by. But few begrudged the bearers their leisure. Fewer still were inclined to trade places with them.

The work was physically demanding. For all of the new destructive technology premiered in the Great War, the battlefront still relied on horse power and human muscle. When moving from the support trenches to the front line, for instance, a Canadian soldier had 60 pounds of kit, clothing, ammunition and rations strapped to his back. In winter the load approached 80 pounds. The soldiers themselves weighed an average of 160; boots and clothing added another 20—more if it was wet. That's the load that two stretcher bearers had to split between them. Even with the help of a shoulder sling, the strain on arms, back, and legs could be unbearable. "You have no idea," one bearer wrote in 1915, "of the physical fatigue entailed in carrying a 12 stone blessé a thousand odd yards across muddy fields."

The work was dangerous. In general terms, those who served in the British Army on the Western Front had a one in three chance of being wounded, and one in eight of being killed. The odds got better or worse according to where you served and what you did. The brunt of the casualties fell on the front line combat troops. The casualty rate for these men has been estimated at sixty per cent or more. The death rate for front line infantry officers was over twenty-five per cent. On the whole, with a casualty rate of eight per cent and a fatality rate of four per cent, the Medical Corps was a safer place to be. But again, the odds varied according to what your job was and where you did it. The Field Ambulances were deployed a mile or less from the front line, and thus were exposed to most of the dangers of the forward trenches. Of the 700-odd men and officers who went overseas with the Field Ambulances, 160 were killed or died of disease, indicating a casualty rate on the same scale as the combat infantry.

The work was stressful. The much-abused infantryman at least got to shoot back every now and then, a psychological release if nothing else. And, when enemy fire came whistling toward them, they could obey their first instinct to dive for cover. Stretcher bearers, if they were in the middle of a "carry," literally had to stand and take it. "Face to face with danger," remembered one British bearer, "the heart beats fast and the sweat oozes from the body, and when the journey is over, sometimes the limbs tremble like young trees in the wind."

It is impossible to even guess at the mental strain involved. There are no accurate statistics for "shell-shock" or "neurasthenia" casualties in the Great War. The British official medical history estimated eighty thousand cases—a two per cent figure that most modern historians dismiss as impossibly low. Studies conducted in World War II suggested that most combat troops would suffer some sort of breakdown after three to four hundred days in combat. Even taking time off for rest and leave, many troops on the Western Front endured seven hundred days or more in combat. Some of the men in the 1st Division's Field Ambulances served over a thousand days at or near the front line. It's a wonder there were any left by the fall of 1918.

Many Great War memoirs or collections of memoirs feature a description of a single monstrous incident, an episode that, over and above all of the War's other monstrosities, epitomizes the monstrosity of that war. They often involve witnessing a wound—inflicted on a friend, inflicted on a total stranger—so terrible that it stands out in memory years, even decades later. These stories only have two endings. "Finally, mercifully," the teller will remember, "the poor bugger died." Or, "Finally, mercifully, the stretcher bearers took the poor bugger away."

One wonders what single, monstrous incident might stand out in a stretcher bearer's memory. One is almost afraid to find out.

Boyde Beck

Introduction

Mary F. Gaudet

I remember visiting my father in the nursing home one day shortly before he died. It was November 1977. His formidable mind, which had revealed itself to thousands of Islanders in a long and distinguished career as a newspaper editor, had now become confused.

"Do you know me today, Dad?" I asked.

His head turned slightly, and his eyes widened as he peered up at me. "You look familiar," he managed.

In an effort to connect with him on a more personal level, I said, "Dad, do you remember your poem, 'The Ballad of the Stretcher Bearers'?"

He lay very still for a short time. Suddenly, in a cadence well-known to me, he recited the six verses, word for word, as a single tear fell slowly down his cheek.

The poem was sixty years old. He had written it on the battlefields of Europe. Here at the end of his eighty-three years, disconnected from the present, his mind strayed back to an experience that had seared itself on his memory and had shaped his entire future life. It was obvious to me that the Great War still held deep meaning and lucid memories for my father.

From A Stretcher Handle: The World War I Journal & Poems of Pte. Frank Walker is a first-person narrative centred around the life and times of my father, Prince Edward Islander Frank Walker (1893–1977), during his service with the Canadian Field Ambulance, Canadian Medical Corps, from its inception in 1914 until 1919, after the Great War had come to a close.

Frank Walker was twenty years old when "the War to end wars" began in 1914. The younger of two sons, he had been born on Christmas Day, 1893 in Charlottetown, Prince Edward Island, to George and Christina (née MacLeod) Walker. His mother, whose Gaelic roots lay in the Isle of Skye, was twenty-seven years younger than her twice-widowed husband. George Walker, formerly from Glasgow, Scotland, had several grown children from his first marriage, and Frank was actually younger than some of his nieces and nephews.

Like so many Islanders of his era, Frank's older brother Jim emigrated to the United States as a young man, settling in Gary, Indiana. And so, when

George Walker died in 1907, aged eighty-four, his widow and fourteen-year-old Frank were left alone. Christina found employment in a private home in Charlottetown in order to support herself and her son. A few years later, Frank dropped out of high school and went to work in the Bruce Stewart & Company Foundry on Charlottetown's waterfront. Although his formal schooling had come to an end, he continued to educate himself with the classics of world literature. His literary turn of mind would only deepen across the years.

When Great Britain (and so, Canada) declared war on Germany on 4 August 1914, twenty-year-old Frank Walker, a machinist who by his own account was all thumbs, enlisted immediately. Four days later, following his acceptance into the Army Medical Corps, Private Walker began to record his experiences as he embarked on all the "Glory and Adventure of War." The entries began in Charlottetown and followed my father's physical and emotional journey through the months of training in Canada and England into the "red confusion" of battle at Ypres, Vimy, Festubert, Givenchy, and Courcelette. Originally captured on scraps of paper, sometimes in the trenches, most often by candlelight, his account was sent home to his mother for safekeeping. Unwittingly, but, perhaps, inevitably, the entries also charted his gradual transformation from military innocent to war-weary veteran. In the summer of 1917, his enthusiasm and idealism spent, Frank gave up recording his impressions. "I grew tired of making notes on every trivial occasion," he wrote, "and the novelty of writing about Active Service can no longer inspire my efforts."

In July 1919, after his demobilization, my father transcribed his accumulated chronicles to create his handwritten War Journal. Besides grouping the scattered entries into a connected narrative, he provided descriptive subheadings. Although there is no way to be sure, lacking the original scraps that he had mailed home, he probably took the opportunity to polish and, possibly, edit his account. In a sense, then, the Journal is twice-filtered: first, in the initial editing of actual experience into a form that would not unduly pain his beloved mother, who was receiving them, and then, in the literary shaping by a natural writer with the time to reflect on what he had written earlier. It, however, has not been published until now.

In addition to the collected entries, the War Journal included personal photographs and newspaper clippings of the day. It also contained a booklet of my father's poetry, *Flanders from a Stretcher-Handle*, which he had published in England during the War. It has been said that Dad got his first taste of printer's ink in the trenches, when he contributed to the Medical Corps' news-sheet, *The Iodine Chronicle*. Perhaps there he received encouragement for his verse or for his long-time dream of becoming a reporter.

The version of the Journal that follows here also incorporates several unpublished war poems that were written into the bound original. Together with the published verse, they essentially represent my father's poetic output. While the informal, personal style of his narrative has a certain reserve to it, the emotion that is often masked in his prose finds expression in his poetry. Employing traditional poetic forms, such as the ballad and sonnet, he writes very striking verse, ranging in mood from the sombre to the ridiculous. Curiously, he does not appear to have written any poetry after the War, except for the sonnet "The Old Battlefield," which was written in 1920 in Charlottetown. Perhaps his subsequent career as a reporter and editor provided the creative outlet that he needed.

Although he was largely self-taught, my father's voracious reading enabled him, in spirit, to travel widely, and his imagination was clearly sparked when seeing places that he had known only from books. As a result, his journal entries weave colourful threads of history and literature into the black cloak of war. His descriptions of military life are intensified by his astute powers of observation and his close attention to detail. And, of course, the Journal leads us, inevitably, into combat, for the War is, after all, the dark heart of his experience.

This publication respects the author's preferences in punctuation: capitals are used freely in unusual places throughout the script, presumably for emphasis; commas and semicolons followed by dashes are also standard punctuation in both his prose and the poetry.[1] A few idiosyncrasies of spelling have been corrected, and all footnotes are editorial additions. Historian Boyde Beck has generously contributed an essay that provides important context about the Canadian Medical Service on the Western Front and a measure of commentary about how my father's Journal fits within that context.

Over the years the spellings for some of the small towns and villages in France and Belgium have changed. I have used the forms from the Michelin Road Atlas of France, Sir Andrew Macphail's *Official History of the Canadian Forces in the Great War, 1914–1919: The Medical Services*

[1.] Interestingly, this style of combining a comma or semicolon with a dash is also employed in the 19th-century "Legend of Salisbury Plain," found in *The Ingoldsby Legends, or Mirth and Marvels*, a short quote from which is included in the Journal.

(Ottawa: Minister of National Defence, 1925), and a few confirmations from Great War scholar Dr. Peter Liddle, Leeds University, UK.

My father's testimony of war has instilled in me a new and deeper respect for the foot soldiers of World War I. It is my hope that it will encourage a greater appreciation for all veterans and victims of war. Quite unexpectedly, the Journal has also given me a unique gift: a charted journey into the youthful heart and soul of its author, the man who was destined to become my father.

Mary F. Gaudet
Charlottetown, Prince Edward Island
September 2000

A War Journal

By Frank Walker

Private; Canadian Field
      Ambulance. A.M.C.

1st Canadian Contingent.

VOLUNTEERS FROM No. 9 A.M.C. FOR OVERSEAS SERVICE   CRASWELL PHOTO

Taken at Charlottetown Armories before departure for the Front, August 1914.

Standing: Frederick Murphy, Charlottetown; John Mortimer, Charlottetown. Seated, left to right: James Ford, Charlottetown; J. Perrault, St. Henri, Montreal; Arthur Phillips, Charlottetown; Frank Walker, Charlottetown; John K. Lacey, Blooming Point, PEI.

1914—(fourth day of the War)
Charlottetown, P.E. Island

Aug. 8

Since the outbreak of War—four long, unendurable days ago—I have
been on pins and needles. Will they take me?—that's the question. It is
maddening to think of those thirty thousand "chosen ones" marching away
to Glory and Adventure—leaving me to drudge my life out in this sordid
old machine-shop.—And all for the want of an inch or two around the
chest!

Thank Heaven! All fears are over now. I have PASSED. I have bearded
the examining doctors in their dens—and come away triumphantly. They,
after much testing and tapping of my anatomy, have solemnly declared
me "Fit for Active Service."

I have now enlisted in the Army Medical Corps, "for service overseas,"
"for the duration of the war and six months afterwards if necessary": solemnly declaring myself to be "of age, and of sound mind, etc., etc."

Aug. 10

Started this morning on Regular Army Pay: $1.00 plus 75¢ Ration Allow-
ance. We drill mornings and afternoons at the armouries, and "await further orders."

Recruiting is going on steadily throughout the Island. Parading troops
are an everyday sight. Victoria Park is resplendent with red and blue and
gold-laced uniforms. Crowds of spectators watch our daily drills. This
unusual solicitude has gone to our heads, quite a bit. We strut around,
for the most part, as if the destiny of the Empire hung on our every step.—
Ridiculous, of course; but there is something grand about it.

August, 1914—Off for the Training Camp

Aug. 17

We entrained this morning for Quebec, where the Contingent will be
mobilized. The date of our departure was not generally known, about
town, but yet quite a crowd of people—friends and well-wishers—had
assembled at the Station. We rode away to a great chorus of cheers, which
we answered. And all along the Line, at every Junction and Station, cheers
and hand-clapping followed until out of sight. For myself, now that the

Mrs. George Walker (née Christina MacLeod), September 28, 1919.

"Great Adventure" has really been embarked upon, I feel sober enough. Poor Mother, I know, will cry for hours. "God keep her and comfort her"—is the prayer of my heart.

Out of the twenty-six medical corps men examined by the doctors, only seven have passed. Our Roll is as follows: Sergeant A. Phillips, Privates: Lacey, Mortimer, Ford, Perrault, Murphy, and Walker. It is understood that we will have to pass further medical tests, as the number of Recruits is yet too great.

August, 1914—Valcartier Camp

Aug. 22
We arrived this morning at Valcartier Camp, the mobilization point. There are some 12,000 troops already here. The place is an ideal one for a camp. It is a great rolling tract of country, fifteen miles from Quebec City. The Laurentian Hills are all around us.

Aug. 30
This is the Life! Open air and weather, plain food, and calm, cool nights under canvas! We go every day on long route-marches over the hills, and come back tired, hungry, and inconceivably happy. In the afternoons, we can go swimming in the Jacques Cartier River, getting back in time for Tea. God bless the cooks!

Fresh troops are pouring in every day. The clamour of drums and bugles and bagpipes can be heard at all hours. The camp-grounds have undergone wonderful changes. What was, but a few days ago, a wilderness of trees and rough plains, has now become a veritable Canvas City, with broad boardwalks, good roads, electric lights, dozens of canteens and stores, and even a couple of Picture Shows.

Aug. 31
We are now,—the seven of us,—definitely joined to a new Unit which is being made up, under the command of Lieut. Col. A.E. Ross, of Kingston, Ontario. It is to consist of Medical Units drawn from all the Eastern Provinces, and will be known as: No. 1 Canadian Expeditionary Field Ambulance.

Sept. 2
We passed our second—and final—Medical Examination today with flying colors. We're well away! Received the first Typhoid inoculation.

Sept. 12

Got the second Typhoid dose yesterday. Feel pretty sick with it. Some of the boys are refusing it. But the doctors assure us that only those who are thoroughly inoculated will be taken to the Front.

September, 1914—Last Days In Camp

Sept. 17

Drill and discipline are now becoming more thorough. The old-style Dress uniforms have been discarded and all hands are in Khaki. Sunday afternoons are our happiest holidays. Then we dress up our neatest, and greet the thousands of visitors who come from all over Canada to see "the boys." On these occasions, camp is a gay place indeed.

Sept. 19

Phillips and I secure a twenty-four's Leave this morning, and visit Quebec City. Having a swell time of it. Everybody wants to "treat" the soldiers. Their hospitality in most cases takes a "liquid" form, and we are being loved "not wisely, but too well!"

Phillips has been reduced to the Ranks (although a fully qualified Sergeant) for no other reason than that there are already too many non-commissioned officers. We Islanders are so small a handful among the other troops, that we expect to get the rough end of the stick for a while; for this reason, we'll see that we hang together.

Captain Duval, a French-Canadian from Saint John, N.B., has been placed in command of our Section. From what I have seen of him already, he's the man for the job. What he doesn't know about Army Regulations, he fills in with common sense. And he understands men.

Sept. 21

A grand Review was held this morning, the whole contingent marching past the saluting stand, where His Highness, the Duke of Connaught, and Col. Sam Hughes, and Premier Borden, were stationed. We looked good, too.

Everything is ready now. The three Brigades, with Artillery, Service Corps, Medical Corps, etc., are up to full strength. Arms, uniforms, and equipment, complete. We will probably go to England for further training. The War appears to be progressing slow enough. Hope it doesn't wind up before we get across.

The Field Ambulance Corps, to which we belong, is composed of

240 men, divided into three Sections (A, B, + C). Each of these Sections is subdivided into "Tent (or Hospital Staff) Division," "Stretcher Bearers' Division," and "Sanitary Division." We carry with us, as officers, eight Doctors; besides a Transport officer and Pay-Master. Our equipment consists of Ambulance Wagons (which we will change for cars when we get to the Front), Bandages of all kinds, Medical Cases, Stretchers, etc.,—a fully equipped unit, able to march with the Infantry, and set up a Field Hospital anywhere, at short notice.[1]

September, 1914—The Contingent Sails
Sept. 26
We break camp this morning, entrain for Quebec, and board the S.S. *Megantic*—one of the great fleet of Ocean Liners which is to take across Canada's first Army. Everybody happy.

Sept. 27
We are now anchored in the St. Lawrence, midway between Lévis and Quebec. Both cities can be seen to fine advantage from the ship. On the Quebec side especially, the view is grand and beautiful. It is dark now, and high up on the cliff can [be] seen the lighted windows of the Chateau Frontenac. The water is all aglow with their reflection. The buzz of a distant train, the intermittent splash of an oar in the river—these are the only sounds that reach us. We stay a long while on deck, gazing across at the twinkling lights, thinking of—a great deal, perhaps, but saying little.

Oct. 1
We awoke this morning to find ourselves in Gaspé Bay. A grey mist hangs over everything and completely hides the shore.

Oct. 2
The fleet is all together now. It is intended we shall cross in one large convoy. The simple Gaspé fishermen must be surprised indeed to see such an Armada in their waters.—It is a sight they will never forget.

---

1. Sir Andrew Macphail's *Official History Of The Canadian Forces in the Great War, 1914–1919: The Medical Services* (Ottawa: Minister of National Defence, 1925), VI, 69, describes the Field Ambulance as being a completely mobile unit which moves with the front line and operates immediately behind it on advance or in retreat. Macphail says that the design and quality of the vehicles are a matter of urgent importance and, at the beginning of the War, horsed ambulances alone were used.

Oct. 3

Leaving Gaspé Bay at noon, we are gradually emerging again into the Gulf. Like an army on the march, the ships now fall into line, making three long columns, a half-mile apart. Cruisers guard the flanks, front, and rear.

(8 P.M.) We are still running slow, to avoid accidents. All the ships are in darkness, with but one mast-light showing.

Oct. 4

We're speeding up a bit now. Passed Bird Island. Cape Roy can be seen some twelve miles to port.

Oct. 5

One of the second-column steamers blows four whistles—"Man Overboard!" Rescued after some difficulty, but too late. What an unfortunate time to be drowned!

Oct. 6

Just clearing the Great Banks off Newfoundland. A gale is coming on, and the ships are tossing like corks in the swell. Seasick.

Oct. 8

Fresh northwesterly winds now, and calm weather. The usual Routine Drill has been started, on Deck. We have the 2nd Class Smoker for a concert-room.

The *Megantic* is carrying about 2,000 troops, in all. The Units are: The 48th Royal Highlanders, The 1st Divisional Ammunition Column, The 1st Field Ambulance, and No. 1 Clearing Hospital. The Highland Pipers keep up a continuous hubbub—which, a mile or two away, perhaps, would sound like music—We are too near the wind-bags to enjoy it much.

October, 1914—At Sea

Oct. 12

We are now approaching the coast of Ireland, and according to everybody, must expect "rough weather." Two French gun-boats joined the convoy this morning. This evening we gathered for the farewell concert in the Smoking-cabin. The usual songs were sung, but when we rose to "The Maple Leaf" and "O Canada!"—the words seemed to have a new and deeper meaning for us all.

The Castle Pipers

1

To hear the Castle Pipers play
It sets me all athril,
It stirs desires, like Gypsy-fires
When marching down a hill.

2

—When marching down a hill at morn
Thro' leafy lanes where birds are waking
On youth's rejoicing step up-borne,
The early way a' taking.

3

To hear the Castle Pipers play
It sets old memory recalling
Boy-dreams of drums and battle's bray,
And charging men, and standards falling.

4

High on the Castle's cloudy verge
Wrapt in the mist, the Pipers play
The "Pibroch" sounds, the "Mountain Dirge"
Then "Scots Wha' Hae!"

5

I see them pace, in regal grace,
The tartaned Chiefs of song and story,
Looking to me, calling to me,
Waving their banners gory!

6

"Souls of my Gallie sires unshriven,
Knights of the plain and blood stained moss
I too have on a red Field striven
And borne a Fiery Cross!"

October, 1914—Nearing England

Oct. 14

We met the "rough weather" all right, but it wasn't as bad as it was cracked up to be. We're getting into sheltered waters now.

(8 A.M.) Land's End sighted on the port bow. As we draw towards the English Channel, the ships spread, and make full speed ahead. The *Megantic, Royal Edward,* and *Franconia* are leaving the others far in the rear.

(11:30 A.M.) The Eddystone Lighthouse is in view. We pass three French merchant ships; also an ancient old square-rigged sailing vessel — reminding me very much of an old print I remember seeing of *The Flying Dutchman* in one of Marryat's sea-tales. The mainland is plainly in view now. Falmouth is visible in the distance.

(1:30 P.M.) We pass an outgoing fleet of British torpedo-boat destroyers. Also pass within hailing distance of a Dreadnaught. The sailors, in white blouses and bare feet—are massed on deck to greet us. A band somewhere strikes up "O Canada." We shout ourselves hoarse.

(3:30 P.M.) We are entering Plymouth Sound. Words fail to describe the scene along the Basin from Plymouth to Devonport. The channel is quite narrow, and winds along in many turns. On both sides, the wharves and roofs of buildings are black with cheering crowds. Bands are playing. The fussy little tugboats, even, are tooting all they can from the Channel, as if to join in the general celebration. As the big ships are slowly brought to moorings, the noise increases to pandemonium. Everyone seems to have gone mad,—and we on the ships are maddest of all.

(6 P.M.) We are now moored in the Channel, off the Naval Dock Yards. The skeleton of some mighty ocean-beast is towering up right before us. Workmen, like the pygmies in *Gulliver's Travels,* are scrambling up and down, hither and thither, pounding its mighty ribs into shape, and looking, in their diminutiveness, almost laughable. Other large vessels are "coaling up" at no great distance. On our way up the Sound we passed some types of the ancient wooden Man O' War (such as Nelson sailed). These "old dogs" are now very useful as training ships. From the poet's or artist's viewpoint, they are priceless.

Oct. 15

The weather continues fine. We continue hanging about the deck-rails, sighing vainly for a Shore-Leave.

The Old Timer

[Extracted from the pages of the Haigville Herald (A.D.
1972) and produced here as a Timely Warning to sundry
gentlemen.]*

A war-scar'd fanatic resides in an Attic
    Above Murphy's Bar, down the street;
He lives on hard-tack, which he keeps in a sack,
    And he sleeps on a cold rubber sheet.

Though grey hair'd and old, there are strange stories told
    Of his dubious habits and ways:
For a bottle of booze he will peddle his shoes,
    And he goes without washing for days.

He gambles, he bets, he accumulates debts;
    And when creditors get on his track
He camps on our lawn, with his gas helmet on,
    And coolly awaits the attack.

Some say he is "barmy"—he'd served in the Army (!)
    And from the Great War had come back
To the cronies he knew, with a gold stripe or two,
    And a few souvenirs in his pack.

O, the stories he tells, and the fond way he dwells
    On the blood-curdling deeds he had done!
(And the deeds are all swore by the notches galore
    He's got on the butt of his gun.)

...continued

---

*   Here, Frank Walker anticipates what might be written about a World War I veteran
many years in the future. In a handwritten copy of this poem found in the journal,
Frank Walker has introduced the poem as follows: "A ballad supposed to be written
about the year 1970 A.D."

October, 1914—We Arrive!
Oct. 16
Tugged to Dock this morning. Now begins the hardest job under the sun.
Unloading ship. It is finally accomplished, however, and we "fall in" on
the pier and march to the Station. Here again, all along the way, are smiles
and cheers of welcome. Thousands throng the streets to see the "Can-oi-
i-i-deans" go by.

October, 1914—The New Camp-Ground
Oct. 17   Salisbury Plain.
De-training at Amesbury this morning, after an all-night ride, and after
marching through about six miles of English lanes, we reach Bustard
Camp, Salisbury Plain. This, we learn, is to be our training ground. Tents,
cook-houses, and all the Camp paraphernalia are already here. But there
are no sidewalks, no electric-lighted Huts for Reading and Recreation, no
Picture Shows—nothing that would allow us for one minute to forget what
we're here for—War training! They say that these camp-grounds have been
used by the Roman Legion. I don't doubt it. If Julius Caesar came back
now he wouldn't find much change. He might notice some barns that had
been re-thatched. Indeed, the whole appearance of the country has, to
our young Canadian eyes, the cast and features of a bygone age. Old clay
cottages, thatched-roofed and gabled-windowed, are plentiful. The neat
brown hedges, lining the country roads and fields, are an agreeable change
to the bare, barbed-wire fences, so often visible on Canadian farms.

The Innocents Abroad
Some few hundred yards from our new "Camp," lies "The Bustard Inn."
This hoary old tavern has seen a hundred and more carousing years pass
away, and still it stands, lusty as ever, by the roadside. "Many the tales
that were told in your top-room, O ancient Inn!" Here came, no doubt,
the soldiers of Wellington, and here they boasted of Waterloo and the
deeds that they had done! Here, in the Inn-parlor of the "Bustard" did we
spend our first memorable evening in Merrie England. We were seated
cozily about the fireplace, mugs of "Ye Olde Ale" at our elbows, pipes and
cigarettes aglow; not, indeed boasting our battle scars but, in other respects,
holding up very well the old traditions.

...continued

All the whiz-bangs he dodged! and the duds which had
     lodged
        But a foot from his fortunate track!
And the shell-holes he filled, with the Germans he killed!
        And the wounded he'd packed on his back!

How he creep'd in the mire, thro' the tangled barb-wire,
        And captured a battery of guns!
And the prisoners he'd made, in a dashing trench raid,
        When he bombed a dug-out full of Huns!

Of course he was there at the Ypres affair,
        Festubert, Givenchy, and Loos!
He'll give you the How, When and Why of each Row,
        Pick out any battle you choose.

'Tis a wonder that he hasn't got a V.C.,
        For all the V.C.'s he had won:
But all of this we don't ask, nor a further bit task
        His mighty Imagination.

October, 1914—Salisbury Plain

Oct. 20

The daily routine—drills and route-marches, are so much like what we went through in Canada that I need describe it no further. Canadian troops are passing through every day, making for other camping-grounds on the Plain. It seems they intend to keep us browsing about these pastures till we are big enough to go to market. We are willing cattle!

Oct. 24

Inspection this morning by Field Marshall Lord Roberts. The weather is wet and miserable. We are lined up along both sides of the Camp road, and the General, with his staff in motor cars, drives slowly through the ranks. He stops often, to speak with Officers and men who are wearing the veteran South African ribbons. He looks decidedly old and feeble. It is marvellous that, at his age, he can run around holding inspection.

Oct. 29

Raining every day. Parades have to be cancelled. We do nothing but hug the insides of our miserable dripping tents.

> "It's a very sad thing to be caught in the rain
> When night's coming on upon Salisbury Plain."
> — *Ingoldsby Legends*[2]

Visited Amesbury this afternoon (spite of the rain). Amesbury is an old village—even for old England. Its ancient name was Ave Bury: it is mentioned in the Legends of King Arthur.

By the roadside, midway between Amesbury and Camp, lies the oldest landmark in Great Britain. This is Stonehenge, the remnant of a Druid temple. The Druids were sun-worshippers, and they flourished in England as far back as 500 B.C. When they built upon the Plains this colossal monument, will never be known. It consists of a pile of gigantic stones—some of them twenty-five feet in height,—planted in circular form on the top of a hill. Some of the stones are standing erect, or leaning, like the Tower of Pisa. Others lie prostrate in the ground, half-hidden in weeds. At all times an impressive sight, this hoary ruin struck us,—returning as we were, along the road after dark, seeing it by "the pale moonlight," and getting the full effect of light and shadow,—it struck in us a feeling of reverence and awe. 'Ere Caesar was born, this ruin of a dead age had been here upon

---

2. Thomas Ingoldsby, Esquire, *Ingoldsby Legends or Mirth & Marvels* (6th ed., London: J.M. Dent & Sons, Ltd. Aldine House, 1930), Introduction, xi. Ingoldsby was a pseudonym used by the Rev. Richard Harris Barham (1788–1845).

Our tent on Salisbury Plain.
Seated: Arthur Phillips, Charlottetown; John K. Lacey,
Blooming Point, PEI. Standing, left to right: Frank Walker,
Charlottetown; J. Perrault, St. Henri, Montreal; J. McDonald,
Montreal; W. Stuart, Montreal; P. Gordon, Montreal;
J. Decormier, Montreal.

the wind-swept Plain! And when we are buried in the dust of oblivion, and forgotten even as the minions and lackeys of Caesar are forgotten today, — these stones will stand. Much poetry has been written upon Stonehenge, but nothing worthy.

Nov. 2

It has turned out fine today, — quite an unusual event in this country I believe. Visited Netheravon — another little close-lying village — this afternoon. Netheravon is important from a military point of view. Besides boasting a Cavalry School, it is the training quarters of a branch of the Royal Flying Corps. We visited the Aerodrome, and spent a pleasant evening with some English troops.

Nov. 4

Inspected today by the King. Fortunately the weather continued clear, and the event came off in first class order. His Majesty was accompanied by the Queen and the Princess Mary. Among the big officials were Roberts and Kitchener — Kitchener's the most regal-looking man I've ever seen. He walks with the stride of an Emperor. The King, alongside him, looks like a lackey. General Alderson, our Corps Commander, conducted the Royal party over the grounds. I heard the King ask, "Are these men really fit?"

Nov. 9

Lord Mayor's Day. — A grand Military Parade takes place in London. Three hundred picked men will represent the Canadian Contingent.

Nov. 10

In place of the usual morning drill, we are now engaged in "sham battles." The Infantry reconnoitre a position, entrench themselves, charge, etc. We follow up with bandages and stretchers. When the "fight" is over, we double forwards and pick up the "wounded." Each wounded man has on his tunic-button a card describing the nature of his wound. We must bandage him accordingly, — as well and quickly as possible, — and carry him back to the Dressing Station, which is pitched in some sheltered nook, a mile or two behind the "field." Here, a Medical Officer is posted, to examine and criticize our work. The afternoons are generally devoted to Route marches — weather permitting. At present state of the roads, this is far from being a pleasant exercise.

Nov. 14

The whole British Empire is in mourning today over the untimely death of Lord Roberts. It seems he had gone to the Front only a few days ago, to inspect his beloved Indian troops. He contracted a bad cold which quickly turned to pneumonia.

Nov. 19

The funeral ceremony for the late Lord Roberts takes place in London today. He will be interred in St. Paul's Cathedral by the side of Nelson, and but a few feet from the tomb of the Duke of Wellington—England's dearest Dust.

Nov. 20

Wet weather continues,—scarcely a day passing without an occasional downpour. The camp-ground is in a terrible mess. We have to keep shifting backward, every week or so, so as not to be submerged. Drill for the present is impossible. A great many are reporting "Sick"—and no wonder. Our feet and clothing are never dry.

The "Princess Patricias" (Canada's crack Regiment) have left the Plains, and are now stationed at Windsor Barracks, London. It is rumored they are preparing for France—lucky devils!

Nov. 22

Newfoundlanders are now encamped on the grounds vacated by the "PPs." They are an exceptionally able-looking bunch of men.

Nov. 27

Army manoeuvres were held today—the whole Division taking part. General Alderson, accompanied by Officers of the Imperial Staff, reviewed us. Mr. Rudyard Kipling, the English poet and novelist, was present too.

It is now fully understood that General Alderson is to take us to the Front. He is already a favorite with the men. Of quiet and gentlemanly appearance, he goes about from camp to camp, making no fuss. He never makes one feel nervous when talking to him,—and he stops often to talk and joke with people—anybody at all—whom he happens to see. The biggest thing about the man is:—he has absolute confidence in us. He tells us often that there's no doubt about it—we're going to make him famous!

Nov. 28

Still raining. We waded—a couple of us—to the hamlet of Shrewton this afternoon, just to kill time. It didn't matter about the rain. We couldn't get any wetter. Spent a not unpleasant evening, in company with some Imperial soldiers and two chubby-faced barmaids.

News has come that the vanguard of Canada's army,—some few Medical Officers and Orderlies,—have landed in France.

December, 1914—Still Raining

Dec. 4

The weather continues favorable for—ducks. But for us,—miserable, shivering, half-drowned, living in a state of unabating mud-soaked misery,—it seems that however bad the Front may be, it can't be so bad, after all!

The Sergeant Major, who seems to be souring more every day, has given up in despair his futile efforts at maintaining any semblance of discipline. We do pretty much as we like, go where we please, and generally one half of the Camp is away on "French Leave" at any given time. The Unit is scattered all over the British Isles. One of the boys went away three weeks ago, leaving the vague address, "Ireland." Of course he will be punished when he returns, but he will probably take it smilingly and "beat it" again, after the next Pay-Day. A few days' "pack-drill," or "Clink" is a cheap price to pay for the luxury of a clean dry bed, baths, and fresh linen.

December, 1914—Camping Under Difficulties

Dec. 5

Phillips, the mechanical genius of our "tent," has just completed the invention of a stove, which he created from the ruins of an old slop-pail, turned upside down, with a hole punched in the bottom for a pipe to enter. This evening we tried it out, with happy results. Fired with some chips, candle-ends, and a few old rags (such as socks, etc.), it makes a glorious blaze. Two of us have volunteered to steal a bucket of coal from the cook-house when the Camp quiets down, and the guard goes to sleep.

All the tents are equipped with oil-stoves, which make a great bluff at giving warmth and heat, but always run dry before they do anything. They are, nevertheless, a great comfort in a tent, for a fellow always imagines that they're giving heat; and, while he's really half-frozen, thinks he's quite warm and cozy, as long as he can see the miserable old wick burning. But our stove has no fake tricks like this. There is no doubt about its heat-

Over The Beer Glass

"He could dress a Wound as neat as any Doc I
    ever saw,
A better Bearer never cuss'd a trench-mat,
He thrived on Pisin Gas; he could drink his Licker
    raw—
But he choked hisself a-tryin' to get the French
    pat."

producing virtue. Two minutes after it was lit, we could warm hands and feet on it; five minutes after, we could toast our bread and make cocoa; within a half-hour we were outside the tent, in the rain, waiting for it to cool off a bit.

Dec. 10
News received today of a glorious victory in the South Atlantic. Four German battle-ships sunk! It is cheering to know they are doing something somewhere. One could sink a German easily in this mud-puddle by the tent-flap. Rain? Holy smoke!

December 1914, London Leave!
Dec. 22
Have just arrived back from London leave—from spending the six most enjoyable days of my life. What a contrast to this muddy dump! Let me retrace my steps, if I can. Catching a motor-lorry at the "Bustard Inn," we quickly left the Camp behind us, and, inside a half-hour, arrived in Salisbury. (Salisbury is worth a longer visit, if only for its fine old Cathedral, and as it is the capital city of Wiltshire, I should certainly have mentioned it long ago. But it was too far away to tempt me.) From Salisbury, we took a train for London, and, after a three-hour journey, arrived at Waterloo Station. It was quite dark then, and we just had time to parade The Strand, "Picadilly," The Mall, Fleet Street, etc., and gape about a bit in the prover-bial rubber-neck fashion.

On the following morning we took a "bus" for Tower Hill, and from thence visited that famous old pile of historic stone work—the Tower of London. We saw everything there that could be seen with the naked eye, (not to mention the tipping fingers). We explored the Armouries, the State-prison cells, saw the Crown Jewels, the Execution block, and the warders, in their quaint Elizabethan costumes. The day was far spent when we finally recrossed the bridge over the moat (now dry), and found ourselves in modern London again.

The next day we saw Westminster Abbey and St. Paul's. To visit the Abbey once, in the right spirit, is to come away wiser and better. I was much interested in the "Poets Corner." Many of the sweetest singers are buried there! Others are represented by busts and medallions. There is no memorial here for Byron. Goldsmith, because he lacked burial expenses, lies elsewhere. How miserable men can be.

Sonnet

My heroes are all Poets! — I have read,—
Yea, unto weariness and waste of time;
Questioning bravoes, knights, and kings long dead,
Following Caesars up through prose and rhyme,
Searching the chronicles of Church and State—
Pondering every name on Glory's Roll,
Eager to prove them all—o simple soul!
What they had never been nor could be—"Great"

Priam was once a King; Nester could see
Future and past; Achilles brooded long;
Hector was brave, and Ajax's arm was strong;—
These were not men for Immortality!
No, but they are immortal, for they be
Amber'd, like flies, in rich, undying song.

As we moved about, through the echoing tombs, I tried to see and remember all that was possible. But this attempt only served to confuse me, and I went out so crowded in mind with thoughts and images that, for the remainder of the day, I could bear no more sightseeing. The Abbey is really so crowded with historic associations that the imagination collapses before them all. The more poetic, or imaginative, one is, the bigger headache he'll have when he comes out—and vice versa. I noticed that one of the fellows, in our bunch, was no more impressed than if he had left an Indian wigwam behind him.

Visited British Museum next day. More head-aches. —Visited Madame Tussaud's famous Wax Work Exhibition, on Baker Street. This was rather disappointing. The figures, true enough, are wonderfully life-like, —but not enough to deceive a critical eye. The "Chamber of Horrors" is but vulgarity gone mad. The Napoleonic relics are the most interesting part of the Exhibition. —At Wellington Barracks, we were priviledged to see the Irish Guards drilling, and the Horse Guards mounting at Whitehall.

The whole six days were ardently spent in sightseeing, and our evenings, in recuperating at various theatres and music halls. I found time to visit Carlyle's house, at Chelsea, also "The Cheshire Cheese," an old Tavern on Fleet Street.

December 1914, Christmas Day—Still Raining
Dec. 25—Christmas Day—A Most Miserable One.
Last night we had a little celebration in the tent, and had left the "Stove" burning merrily when we went to bed. The first thing I realized, on awakening this morning, was that the tent was in flames and that somebody, through a haze of suffocating smoke, was shouting "Fire! Fire!" We subdued the fire, not without hard fighting. The tent was a wreck: much of our blankets and clothing was destroyed. It seems that, during the night, some convivial one had come in, and finding us all asleep, gone out again, knocking over the stove in his exit. He nearly succeeded in broiling us alive.

It was yet an hour before dawn, and the Camp still lay in slumber, when we stole quietly away towards the empty tents of the Medical Depot. There we "lifted" a tent, complete, pegs, pole, canvas and all, and carried it back, erecting it over the now buried remnants of our burnt bedding. To "lift" some blankets from the Store-tent was the work of a few minutes. We were now all right again, and, with many a sigh of thankfulness, so "turned in" for another "nap" before Réveillé.

This morning passes very listlessly. The usual drip-drip-drip overhead. Everyone, I suppose, is thinking what a good time he might be having elsewhere. The officers of the First Brigade have got up for us a Turkey Dinner, to be given this afternoon in the Y.M.C.A. tent. A concert for the evening has been proposed.

Dec. 29
A big wind-storm last night caught up our newly erected horse stables, and blew them all over Camp, leaving the horses to run wild on the Plains. We had to "turn out" for this, and then, an hour later, were forced out of bed to peg the tents down again. And in the meantime it rained. Before such storms as we are having, a canvas tent is about as serviceable as cheese-cloth.

January, 1915
Jan. 1—New Year's Day. Miserable.
We sit, a dismal wet circle, around the creaking tent-pole, listening to the "pat-pat" of the infernal rain on the dripping canvas overhead—"and we would that our tongues could utter—!" It would be risking one's life to quote Longfellow here. But indeed there is no attempt at cracking feeble jokes. We have got beyond that stage of misery. And so the morning drags on! There is nothing to do—no place where one might go to spend a dry hour. Clothes, blankets, bedding—all are sodden. Nobody seems to have any tobacco, and it is a half-hour's tramp through the mud to the nearest Canteen.

Jan. 2
Pay Day! As soon as I drew pay, I caught the first "bus" into Salisbury. Most of the boys were ahead of me there. What luxury! Hot baths, clean clothes, dry sheets to roll in! We feel once more like human beings. The rain has been so severe in these parts that streets in Salisbury—many of them,—are flooded to a depth of three feet, and the old women are going to market on rafts. Even the Cathedral has been flooded out. And Sunday passes, for the first time in thirty years, without a Church service.

Arriving back to Camp, after an unauthorized absence of two days,—quite impenitent—the worthy "O.C." condemns me to the "Clink," there to work out my sentence of "seven days."

Omar In The Clink

Awake! the sun is on the Cinder-path.
     Shake from thee Rum's remorseful aftermath;
The Sergeant-Major with the Crime-sheet waits,
Prepare thy Bluff to soothe the Old Man's wrath.

January, 1915—"The Pity of It"

Jan. 18

A deadly disease, known as Spinal Meningitis, has broken out in Camp. It is caused by unsanitary living, wet feet, over-exposure to cold, etc. It first strikes the kidneys, whence it creeps to the spine and, in fatal cases, affects the brain. There are few such cases at our particular Camp, but on other parts of the Plain the disease is spreading rapidly. Why on earth can't they send us to France, instead of leaving us here to die?

Feb. 2

It is rumored that we shall be off for France soon. Such news, if only for its tonic effect on the spirits, is worth believing. In spite of winter hardships, our Infantry boys are really in fine condition. It is a pleasure to watch them, every morning in clear weather, marching off to the Ranges, drums and bugles going. The General inspects us as regularly as possible.

Feb. 4

Final Inspection this morning by the King and Lord Kitchener. The Camp is in a state of excitement hard to describe.

February, 1915—Off for the Front at Last!

Feb. 7   **Marching orders at last!**

We break camp this morning, amid the usual downpour of rain, and start for Amesbury. The transport teams give all kinds of trouble. Horses balk, wagons stick in the mud, and the rain increases to torrents. But in spite of it all, we're happy enough. Entraining at Amesbury, we proceed to Bristol, and from thence to Avonmouth Dock, where we board the S.S. *Atlantian*.

Feb. 8

The 4th Battalion arrives on board this morning. The day is occupied in loading wagons and stores. The ship is an old cattle steamer. We leave Bristol 6 P.M.

Feb. 10

Seasick. Don't know where we are, we're tossing about like a cork, and have been all day. I thought it was a two hours' run to France! I've been lying in the hold most of the time, not able to keep my feet. The Sergeant Major is here too. At present he is cursing all water with a vehemence and fluency which simply keep the air blue around him. I fear he is a violent man.

(Later) Everybody says we're on the Bay O'Biscay, though what we are doing in this part of the world is beyond me. The sea is still choppy.

(Later) A dim coast-line can be seen now. There are a number of lighthouses jutting out into the sea.

Feb. 11
Weather foggy last night and this morning. We have come to anchor, just inside the harbor of St. Nazaire on the River Loir.

Feb. 12
Taking advantage of the early tide this morning, the *Atlantian* docked. (2 A.M.)

From breakfast time until 3 P.M. we were busy unloading—a job, of all jobs, I detest the most. When all is clear, we "Fall in" and march to the Station. The natives take little notice of us. It seems a customary thing for troops to land here. There is no doubt but we are in the old soil of France. One glance at the quaint, red-tiled house-roofs, and the narrow, crooked cobbled streets, puts one instantly in mind of duelling swords, midnight serenades, and all the romantic background of "The Three Musketeers." There are sailors of all nationalities, lounging about the street corners. In the crowded docks lie every class of ship, from the tiny fishing-smack to the big French-Merchantman—for St. Nazaire is still a very important sea-port. We reach the Railway Station, after a short tramp, and board the waiting boxcars—forty men to a car!

February, 1915—Not There Yet
Feb. 13
All night we have been bumped and tossed about like so many bags of oats. The boys are just waking, and there is much grunting and swearing. Any attempt to stretch cramped limbs ends in disaster—to someone else. We slide the big doors open, and the fresh morning air rushes in, with reviving effect. We are flying along at considerable speed, past sidings and crossings and armed Sentries in bright red and blue uniforms. The sun comes out, beautifully warm.

We stop long enough at our Station to allow for a good "wash-and-brush-up." Everybody happy.

A bad accident. This evening, in one of the cars ahead, a 4th Battalion man fell out, somehow. He was killed under the wheels.

The Red Cross

Bright pledge of Succor!—Christ's own standard flying
Serene, where Hell's mad nightmare-furies rave!
Soothing the fever'd pangs of maim'd and dying,
Steeling the sicken'd heart to firmly brave.
All agonies the spririt is enduring;
Find solace 'neath thine arms, which stretch to save
A beacon point, a harbourage assuring,
Gleaming o'er battle's wild, impassion'd wave!

When these hoarse guns in rusted silence lie
With Kaisers, armies, empires, long unsung,—
Buried among the world's forgotten dust—
Whose praise shall swell the minstrel's melody?
Whose story linger on the pilgrim's tongue?
Lord, keep thy Bearers constant in their Trust!

February, 1915—Arrive at Hazebrouck

Feb. 14

All hands fagged out. We couldn't get any sleep in such bumping and tossing. The train stops occasionally, and we jump out to stretch limbs and drink hot coffee.

(11 A.M.) After passing through a tunnel we reach Bologne. Everywhere here can be seen British and French troops, Red Cross nurses, Ambulance trains, and carloads of provisions and munitions of war.

The country is getting more rugged and picturesque. Tumble-down windmills dot the landscape; old chateaux appear, with towers and turrets. At 12:30 the red-tiled roofs of Calais come in sight. —We are nearer it, I hope, than the Kaiser's legions will ever be!

(3 P.M.) We arrive at our destination—Hazebrouck. The hateful job of unloading starts again. By five o'clock all is clear, and we "Fall in" and march off, through the town, and out into the country, the transport wagons bring up the rear.

After a tramp of eight miles, we manage to lose ourselves in a long, deserted lane, lined with hop-poles[3] and, as night is upon us, it is vain to go further. The Major goes off on a reconnaissance sally, and comes back to lead us to a Billet he has found in a nearby hayloft. We "turn in" thankfully, and soon all hands are snoring under the warm straw in deep and measured cadence.

February, 1915—France

Feb. 15   Meterice.

(This was the village we were looking for last night. We discovered ourselves within a half-mile of it.) The day is spent in cleaning up, and getting settled to our new quarters. Hay barns are an agreeable change from Cattle cars and leaky tents. The sound of distant gunfire is quite audible.

Feb. 18

This billet, and the surrounding country, was, but a short while ago, in the Enemy's hands. Hard fighting took place around this very barn, they say. But there is no sign of shell-fire. There is not much to be seen—or had—around the village. The Germans have looted the country with that thoroughness so peculiar to them.

---

3.   Editor's Note: My brother, John Walker, offers this explanation of hop-poles. In France and Belgium, they grow hops for beer-making. They put up large poles in the ground and then tie ropes from the top of the pole to the ground. They grow hop vines up these ropes. When the hops are ready for harvest, they climb to the top of the poles and slide down the ropes, knocking off all the ripe hop leaves.

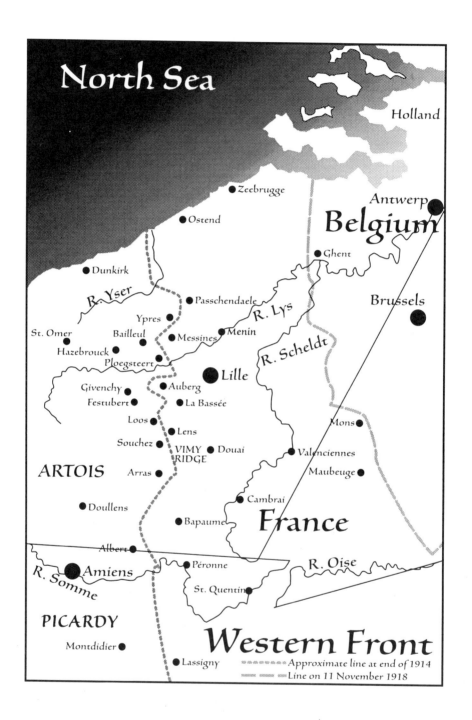

North Sea

Holland

Zeebrugge

Ostend

Antwerp

Belgium

Dunkirk

Ghent

R. Yser

Passchendaele

R. Lys

Brussels

Ypres

St. Omer

Bailleul

Menin

Hazebrouck

Messines

R. Scheldt

Ploegsteert

Lille

Givenchy

Auberg

Festubert

La Bassée

Loos

Lens

Souchez

VIMY
RIDGE

Douai

Mons

Valenciennes

ARTOIS

Arras

Maubeuge

Doullens

Cambrai

Bapaume

France

Albert

R. Oise

R. Somme

Amiens

Péronne

St. Quentin

PICARDY

Montdidier

Western Front

Lassigny

░░░░░░░░ Approximate line at end of 1914
▓▓ ▓▓ ▓▓ Line on 11 November 1918

Feb. 20

The Canadian Contingent was inspected today by Field Marshall Sir John French. He was introduced to our leading Commanders by General Alderson. We have now about 20,000 men in France. The remainder of the Contingent will be kept in England, to form a Base for Re-enforcements.

February, 1915—First Trip to the Line

Feb. 24

The Infantry Battalions are now taking turns in the trenches,—each Company doing a stretch of forty-eight hours duty. It is quite cold in this part of the country now. We have been issued fur jumpers, thick leather mitts, and warm caps with ear-lugs.

Feb. 27   Fleurbaix.

We move up today to within a few kilometres of the Firing Line, where we take over the duties of No. 22 Field Ambulance R.A.M.C.—an English outfit which has been here for several months.

February, 1915—Active Service

Feb. 28

Our present duties appear to be simple enough. The Stretcher Bearers start off, at dusk every evening, in squads of six men, to the Advanced Dressing Stations, which are situated a few hundred yards behind the trenches. There, the wounded are collected and returned to the Main Dressing Station at Fleurbaix. Here, they are thoroughly examined, their wounds re-dressed. Motor cars take them from the Main Station to the Casualty Clearing Station and from thence they go, by train, to the Base Hospitals. The whole system is minutely worked out. My work lies with the Stretcher Bearers. We have two Advanced Posts to attend to, half the party being detailed, each evening, to work together from each post.

One of the Aid Posts is situated on the outskirts of Bois Grenier. This was probably a very fine city—before the War. It is now a pile of ruins, deserted by all save the Sentries on guard at the street crossings, and a few Medical Officers, quartered in old cellars. The tall church tower is still standing, silent and alone, like a monument over the dead. The fiercest of fighting was centred here for months, with apparently little success on either side. Our other Advanced Post is in an isolated cottage, lying in the fork of two roads, and is known as "Y Farm." All traffic to this place must

be made at night, and even under darkness the German searchlights make movements dangerous. From Y Farm a panoramic view can be had of the trench-lines. Star-shells light up the scene in a weird way,—like a stage under spotlights. The trenches run before us roughly in the shape of a gigantic horseshoe. I am told this "curve" in the Line is partly an optical illusion.

Mar. 1

The Germans dropped three nine-inch shells into Fleurbaix this afternoon,—killing one man, and wounding several others. The boys are busy collecting bits of shrapnel splinters and "noses" for souvenirs. For my part, I think we'll see too many of them before long.

Returned this evening from Bois Grenier Aid Post with no wounded. The Line is very quiet.

Mar. 12

Constant and heavy gunfire last night and all this morning. There are some six-inch batteries close by, and nothing can be heard above their deafening roars. A few shells have landed not far from Billet. One of these, failing to explode, is now lying quietly behind the house, buried in the garden. We have orders to leave it strictly alone—of course!

Mar. 15

For the first time since leaving the Plains, we "fall in" for Church Parade. Captain Gordon conducts the open-air Service.

Mar. 16   Sailly-sur-la-Lys.

We left Fleurbaix this afternoon. The Canadians are being withdrawn from the trenches for a few days' rest.

March, 1915—St. Patrick's Day

Mar. 17   St. Patrick's Day.

We celebrated the Anniversary of Ireland's Patron Saint with an open-air concert. Captain Boyce brought forward a dilapidated old phonograph and some records, which he had discovered in the Billet. The records were all in French, of course. It was sweet to hear the old needle scratching, though!

Everyone seems contented, now that we have at last reached our goal. There is an almost brotherly affection existing betwixt us all—from the

France—1915

Like knights, we've quit our Banquet Halls,—
The gong of Time has struck the hour;
And chivalry's again in flower,
And banner waves and trumpet calls.

O Trumpet! calling clear and loud;
That wakes the souls of Sloth and Ease
And blows them over stormy seas,
And shrives them in a battle cloud!

The tombs of unheroic years,—
They moulder in some chapel-nave;
The flowers on the soldier's grave
Are watered with his Country's tears.

By moated walls and sedgy streams
Here on the Towney-fields of France
We're camping out with old Romance
And coining poets' golden dreams.

Estaires
March 1915

dear old Colonel—("Daddy," we call him)—down. We are beginning to understand and appreciate each other. We are all a big family, planted in an alien part of the world, and it's up to us to love each other.

The weather conditions, the work, and the food are much better than we had any reason to expect.

March, 1915—Estaires

Mar. 25   Estaires.

We took over the Rest Camp at Estaires this morning, relieving the 25th (Devon) Field Ambulance. The Camp, or rather Hospital, is situated in a great brick building, presumably a school house or academy. Estaires is quite a large, and very busy, town. Business is going on full swing. Thousands of English and French troops are billeted here, also Gurkas, and a Regiment of the famous Black Watch.

Mar. 27

Whilst at breakfast this morning, two loud explosions shook the building, and brought the window panes about our ears. Rushing outdoors in great excitement, we were in time to see a fast diminishing speck in the sky— which assuredly was the tail of a German bombing plane. The bombs made two nice holes in the garden, behind the Rest Camp. Had they landed any other place in the city, but in this deserted garden, they could not fail to have killed or maimed somebody.

There is a grand old Cathedral in Estaires. The interior is rich with priceless works of art,—paintings, statuary, and stained windows. Adorning the altar and pulpit are magnificent carvings in wood. On the outside, the stone work is beautifully carved. For its historic interest alone, this Church is worth a long visit. Then there is the Town Hall. This is a great, ungainly pile of black brick and stone-work. It stands upon the main street, facing the "Grande Place." A tablet above the arched doorway has the following inscription—"A.D. 1612."

Mar. 30

The Bishop of London (who is touring the Front) gave us a brief address this evening before the Town Hall. Then our "beloved General" rose and spoke a few short but pointed sentences, which we hilariously applauded. The General is so popular a man now, with rank and file, that he draws cheers after him wherever he goes—whether he says anything or not. His serene confidence in us, despite our undisciplined ways (as compared with

April 1915   Mt. De Cats.

The country round about is most
beautiful. We route-marched this
morning to the top of Mt. De Cats,
a great hill rising some five hundred
feet above sea-level. The view
was magnificent. In the
distance lay the Belgian frontier,
and everywhere, close at hand, were
little hamlets and tall church-
spires, half-hidden behind poplar
trees. The red roofs of the house-tops
contrasted pleasingly with the green
and brown of the rich country side.
Great white cobbled highways stretched
themselves into long ribbons over
the hills, and the poplar trees
followed them, until they ran
out of sight, beyond the waving
arms of distant wind-mills.
      As we gazed upon this bit of
old Colew, it was hard to
realize that, but a few miles away,
the guns were roaring and men
were falling in agony.
On the summit of Mt. De Cats is
a Monastry, — a relic of the Middle
ages, — which has been lately turned
into a Hospital. There is also here,
the antique frame-work of a
wind mill, long since superannuated.

English soldiers), and his straightforward manner of speaking when he does speak,—are typical of the whole man.

German planes are again bombing the Town, this time more successfully. One of the Raiders has been brought down by our Anti-craft guns.

April, 1915—On The Move
Apr. 6   Godewaersvelde.

Moving from Estaires this morning on the heels of the 2nd Brigade, we find ourselves, after a twelve-mile tramp, in a straggling Flemish village bearing the above jaw-breaking name. Here we find our billet in the "École," or school house,—a one-storied building of brick, with stone flooring and black-boarded walls, decorated profusely with various antique prints, a couple of obsolete maps of Europe, and a life-size picture of Victor Hugo.

After many vain attempts at pronouncing the name of our village, I found in the end, that, like most riddles, it was quite easy—when you know how. Leaving out all the superfluous letters, it reads like this: "Goderswell," with the accent on the first syllable. Why on earth they stuck in the other vowels is beyond me.

April, 1915—Mont de Cats
Apr. 9

The country round about is most beautiful. We route-marched this morning to the top of Mont de Cats, a great hill rising some five hundred feet above sea-level. The view was magnificent. In the distance lay the Belgian frontier and everywhere, close at hand, were little hamlets and tall church spires, half-hidden behind poplar trees. The red roofs of the house-tops contrasted pleasingly with the green and brown of the rich country side. Great white cobbled highways stretched themselves into long ribbons over the hills, and the poplar trees followed them, until they ran out of sight, beyond the waving arms of distant windmills.

As we gazed upon this bit of Old Eden, it was hard to realize that, but a few miles away, the guns were roaring and men were falling in agony.

On the summit of Mont de Cats is a Monastery,—a relic of the Middle Ages,—which has been lately turned into a Hospital. There is also, here, the antique framework of a windmill long since superannuated.

Thro'...The Mists of the Mornings

—"and they came,—singing as they
came,— marching through the
mists of the morning."
—Old Song

Out of the grey of breaking day
    Shadowy forms espy,
Tramping the rough, white cobbled way,
    Under the poplars high.

Tramp, tramp, tramp, thro' the mists they come,
    Shouting in care-free song,
Timing their feet to the sturdy drum,
    Swinging their arms along.

Tramp, tramp, tramp, by the old brown mill
    And the red roof'd cotts they go;
On to the crest of the rising hill,
    Over the plain below.

The mandate call of the drum is borne
    Far on the eager breeze,
Rousing to echoes the listless morn,
    Stirring the drowsy trees.

...continued

April, 1915—Signs of Trouble

Apr. 17 **Chateau grounds, near Brelin.**

I am temporarily transferred, along with another Ambulance man, to the
Army Service Corps. Our duties consist in drawing the daily rations at the
Ordinance Stores and delivering them, through the Service Corps, to our
own Unit. The Field Ambulance is stationed now at Watou. Our lines
here, at Brelin, are quite near the famous town of Ypres. Just beyond Ypres,
heavy fighting is going on. The roaring of our own guns is continuous and
nearly deafening. The trenches are quite three miles away, but the shelling
here is bad at times. German aeroplanes are almost constantly overhead.

Apr. 18

The heavy gun-fire continues. We are getting teams hitched, ready for the
long drive to Watou. The shelling has not touched our area so far.

April, 1915—The Battle of Ypres

Apr. 20

The fighting of the past few days has resulted in the capture of Hill 60,
a strong position two miles southeast of Ypres. The Germans continue
counter-attacking. Here, directly behind the Line, everything is in a state
of excitement. The Ypres-Poperinghe Road is packed with advancing columns of troops,—with cars, lorries, ammunition limbers, and all the paraphernalia of War. Civilians, old and young, are flying from the surrounding villages. The German shell-fire is hourly growing heavier. We are still
in a comparatively safe position. Our own First Brigade is in billets near
Poperinghe,—just behind us. Troops of Infantry and Cavalry are quartered
everywhere, for miles behind the Lines.

Apr. 22

The fighting has increased in fierceness to a regular battle. The Germans
are reported to have broken our Lines, and are making towards Calais. We
move our transport wagons to a safer position, behind Poperinghe. Driving
back from Brelin this evening, after we had delivered our Ration load, we
met our own Ambulance Stretcher Bearers going into the Line. We felt
sore, too, that we were not going—but "Orders is Orders!" I think Joe (the
other fellow) takes this disapointment harder than I do.

...continued

Nature's gentle Reveillé sounds,
  Dawn is retiring far,
And Day is making his early rounds,
  Guarded by one tired star.

The sun's astir on the grey church towers,
  Lighting his lamps again
In the dewy globes on the hop-vine bowers,
  On clover, and leaf, and grain.

But the mists are thick, and the wild weed waves
  Where their restless feet contend:
Behind the mists are the scattered graves,
  Marking the journey's end.

Godewaersvelde, 1915

Apr. 23

Excitement is rising to frenzy. No one seems to know exactly what is going on. The wounded who have come in report a terrible engagement taking place near St. Julien, in which we are distinctly getting the worst of it. Some say the Germans have broken through the French Line, and so have surrounded the Canadians altogether. Others report that Fritz is sending over clouds of gas, which kill every breathing thing for miles around. We are nearly crazy with anxiety for our own boys.

Delivered Rations this morning as usual. The Tent Division of the Ambulance Corps is stationed at Vlamertinghe. Here, the wounded are pouring in by the hundreds. Those who could walk have limped as best they could, from the trenches. Others crawl in, helped along by comrades. The roads are blocked with Ambulance cars. Wounded men are lying on stretchers, outside the Dressing Station, along the high-road, in fields, and on the doorsteps of houses. Doctors and Orderlies are working as quickly as possible, but the queues of waiting wounded are steadily growing longer and more unmanageable. We pleaded with Captain Boyce to be allowed to go up with the Stretcher Bearers. But he couldn't allow that, as there is no one to relieve us here.

Apr. 24

The fighting is still going on. There is not much reliable news from the Front. The Germans have been shelling Poperinghe and Vlamertinghe all morning. I guess our Dressing Station will have to be shifted. The civilian inhabitants have all cleared out, leaving homes in disorder.

Apr. 25

The battle continues. It is feared our Infantry regiments have been annihilated. Engineers are busy night and day erecting trenches, block houses, and barbed-wire entanglements over the whole stretch of country between Ypres and Poperinghe.

Apr. 26

Infantry, Cavalry, and Artillery re-enforcements are coming up, by the thousands. What's left of our own boys are being withdrawn from the trenches. Our Stretcher Bearers are back again, after three days and nights' steady work in the Line. They had no sleep, and very little to eat. Phillips tells me it all seemed a nightmare, but can describe nothing of his experience. Our own casualties were very slight—two killed and six wounded, I believe. This would be among a hundred men. The Infantry casualties were, in

some cases, as high as 80 per cent. We lost one motor car and two horse ambulances in the shell-fire. The Canadian casualties altogether will come to near ten thousand,—nearly 50 per cent. Captain Duval—our Section Commander, is seriously wounded. Also the Transport Officer, Capt. McGibbon.

Our position is now secure; but that it was actually hanging in the balance, and that our boys, by their pluck in sticking to the trenches until relief came, actually saved the day,—there can be no doubt.

May, 1915—Aftermath

May 2
(Sunday) Wounded are still coming in to the Dressing Station, but the battle is, for the present, over. The Field Ambulance has moved back again to Watou.

May 3
The Germans are again shelling Poperinghe, evidently feeling about for the areodrome. A farm laborer at Menin has been arrested for suspicious conduct and proven a German spy.

May 5   Bailleul.
The Canadian Brigades are being moved from the Ypres Salient. We will be kept here, likely, for rest and re-enforcements.

May 10
Papers are full of the horrible news of the torpedoing of the American ship *Lusitania*. This should be convincing to a "neutral" world. To the Germans, there is no such word as "neutrality." "Those who are not for us are against us," quoted the Kaiser, in a memorable speech. And America can not save herself by standing aside.

May 11
Yesterday evening at St. Paul's, London, a Memorial Service was held for the Canadians killed at Ypres. The Bishop of London conducted the Service, and paid our boys a touching tribute. What a noble thing to die in a blaze of glory like this! Many of these boys might have lived on to mean and sordid old age. But now they are forever young.

"Sinking to rest —
By all their Country's wishes blest."

Through Old Bethune

We marched one day through old Bethune
      In columns northward veering;
Our feet in step, our hearts in tune,
      Our singing drowned in cheering.
We saw the flags from house-tops flung
      The maids from windows peering,
The doors agape with old and young,
      The children wild careering.

And now we march through grey Bethune
      With drum-sticks mutely lying!
No foot's in step, no heart's in tune,
      No song is worth the trying.—
Oh, Ypres was a bloody fray
      We left our comrades dying,
The comrades who had marched so gay
      When all the flags were flying.

Flanders 1915

General Alderson is torn between grief over the casualties, and pride in the knowledge that his "boys" are all he thought them to be. It was his own self-confidence which inspired the men, and produced such glorious results.

May, 1915—New Scenes

May 14
A long hike across hills has landed us in the little village of Callone,—three or four cottages, a church, and two Estaminets make up the village. We find our billet, as usual, in a hayloft.

May 20   Hinges.
Another move this morning. We are now within three miles of Bethune,—a big town which we must see, as soon as Pay-Day comes around.

The weather is beautifully fine and warm, crops and flowers are up already. It is like mid-summer in Canada—though not so scorchingly hot. We have abandoned the stuffy old billets in haylofts and houses, and are camping out in bivouacs and roughly made tents, spread in the fields. All hands are sun-tanned and "fit" as the proverbial fiddle.

I enjoyed, this afternoon, a "dip" in the cool waters of the River Lys. After the hot march from Callone it was a double treat. The Lys River is a sort of natural Canal, which winds through a great part of Northern France, and carries commerce to and fro continually. It is fresh-water.

May, 1915—Battle of Festubert

May 31   Busneltes.
Our Bearers have again been through the "Mill," but escaped without casualties. We arrived here today after a tiresome march. Bivouac for the night in open fields. The big town of Lillers is close by.

June 13
The Battalions are being issued Lee Enfield rifles to replace the Canadian Ross. Many lives were needlessly wasted over this rifle-question, which should have been settled before we ever came to the Front. The Ross rifles are good for sniping, but useless for quick firing.

Stretcher bearer: McBriarty, Saint John, NB.

June, 1915—Battle of Givenchy

June 15

Heavy gun-fire has been going on, for the past two days, in the direction of La Bassée. We start this evening for Givenchy in Stretcher-squads, by motor car.

June 20

Having at last come personally through a real battle, I find my ideas of it very confused. I cannot distinguish well between what I saw and what I only imagined seeing. At any rate there was very heavy shell-fire. On the morning of the 16th, at 2 o'clock, we reached Givenchy. We waited all day by the railway lines, on the banks of the Canal. About 6 P.M. we were sent up to the Advanced Aid Post, and continued carrying, back and forth to the Embankment, with short intermissions for eating, until the wounded were well cleared away, and the fighting had died down. We are now resting up at the sand-pits, Beuvry.

June, 1915—Bailleul Goodbye!

June 25   Outside Bailleul.

We broke camp in the evening of the 23rd, and a long night's march carried us into Estaires-du-nord. Last night we again took the road and after eight hours marching, we have halted here for the day. All hands are tired out and grousing.

Jul. 11

We had, after all, a good fortnight's stay in Bailleul. This was a piece of luck "devoutly to be wish'd." Bailleul is a fine city, with Estaminets galore, all kinds of pretty girls, etc., etc. We are now moved up into Belgium again,—to a little village called Romarin.

August, 1915—Trenches at Ploegsteert

Aug. 4

Am sent up, this evening from Romarin, along with six other Bearers, to our Advanced Dressing Station in Ploegsteert Wood (Plug Street, the boys call it). This Dressing Station is a well-built—and sandbagged—log hut, situated in the woods behind Hill 63. Another similar hut shelters the Medical Officers and staff, and a third and smaller one serves for cook-house. The village of Ploegsteert lies a mile or so away.

Bob Ross, our cook—famous for his bully-beef stews.

Aug. 5

The line is very quiet here. We may wander unchallenged along the communication trenches, and right into the Front Line. The German trenches lie some two hundred yards away, hidden by the crest of a hill. The field guns pop off occasionally, and, at long intervals, one hears the sharper crack of a rifle. That is all. It is hard to think of this as being a battlefront.

A few days ago Premier Borden paid us a visit. He was accompanied by Prince Arthur of Connaught. Not to be beaten, I suppose, General Sam Hughes is now making the rounds.

August, 1915—Ploegsteert Wood

Aug. 11   At the Aid Post of the 8th Battalion, Ploegsteert Wood.

I was much interested, this afternoon, in watching the manoeuvres of one of our air-men. For an hour he has been patrolling the Line, changing his position and elevation continually to keep out of range of the German gunners, who are deliriously firing all about him. He managed his machine with the skill of a wizard. This spectacle is, of course, a daily occurrence here. But I cannot get over the wonder of it. Often we have to dive for shelter when our own anti-aircraft guns are firing, as the shrapnel bullets fall everywhere. They land with a force sufficient to bury them six inches in hard ground.

The Aid Post here is situated along the main road, above "Hyde Park Corner"—a name given it by some homesick Tommy.

Aug. 15 —1st Battalion Aid Post.

A hard night. We are at the Aid Post known as "Gloucester House," on the "Strand," situated about a mile from the Dressing Station. Our path runs through dense wood and along a road thick with mud from yesterday's rain, and pock-marked with shell-holes. At night, it is a two hours' job to fetch a case out.

The "Strand" is a narrow board walk running through Ploegsteert Wood. It was famous in the early days of the War when men spoke, with grim humor, of "Plug Street."

Aug. 29

Relieved this morning by other squads of Bearers. We return to the Unit Headquarters at Romarin. News has come from England that our dear Section Commander, Captain Duval, is dead. He succumbed to the wounds received at Ypres.

Taken at Romarin on the Belgium-France frontier, fifteen kilometres behind the Line. All Islanders! Frank Walker is standing on extreme right with pipe.

September, 1915—Neuve Église

Sep. 4

I was in Neuve Église this afternoon, with others on a fatigue party, loading brick for our new transport lines. The Germans began shelling, and we stood not upon the order of our going, but went at once. Of Neuve Église, a once lovely town, not a single house is standing whole. There is yet one inhabitant there, an old, old woman, who insists on sticking to her little cottage, despite the fact that buildings on both sides of her are in ruins. When the shelling starts, she creeps into the cellar. She is so deaf that she can hear nothing until something falls down, or the soldiers on duty arouse her. What misery has been thrown upon the closing years of this poor creature's life!

September, 1915—Romarin

Sep. 17   Romarin.

The Camp is visited at times,—when we are off on Parade or elsewhere,—by a carnivorous old cow, who tramps about the grounds "seeking what she may devour." She noses under tents and bivouacs, and eats up all the rations. Today this creature has added yet another outrage, which brings forcibly home to us the fact that "out-door life" has its little disadvantages. In our "Bivy," well-hidden under kitbags and blankets, we had stored a bag-full of nice ripe corn, (stolen from a nearby farm) and two rolls of fresh butter. The corn was to be the occasion of a "Big Feed" this evening. We had invited friends and conspirators from all directions, to swell the happy occasion. But we reckoned without that Cow!

Sep. 18

The 2nd Canadian Contingent is now in France. General Alderson will be in full command. Our worthy Colonel (Daddy) has been promoted A.D.M.S. and Major Wright is taking command of the Ambulance Corps. We are all sorry for this. The Colonel has been a father to us all, and, if he ever had to punish us, it was "more in sorrow than in anger." He was almost too lenient. But what a virtuous failing!

Sep. 25

Grave-digging this morning, in the little bit of "God's Acre" behind the Dressing Station. We have planted maple seeds here, and some day it will be beautiful. There are thousands of little cemeteries such as this, scattered behind the Lines, and it is our sad privilege to tend them.

Last Post

Farewell! Farewell!
      Our comrade dear, we leave you.
Your camp ground lone
Will bear no stone,
And none may come to grieve you.

A thought—sweet thought!
Shall comfort us who love you:
Around your bed
The dank weeds spread;
—The sky spans clear above you!

Soon Spring will bring
The birds to carol o'er you;
And every wind
That blows will find
Its hymnal music for you.

Sep. 27

Big French success. The British have captured Loos. Here, behind the Ploegsteert Front, everything is quiet. One would scarcely know a War was on, but for the occasional booming of the guns.

Oct. 4

English troops are taking over this part, and we are packing up, ready for the march.

October, 1915—Bailleul Again

Oct. 9   Bailleul.

We are well-settled here for the winter. The Field Ambulance has taken over the Rest Hospital and comfortable billets have been allotted us. Bailleul is much as it was in pre-war times. Business goes on uninterrupted by the stray bombing-raids, and at night, behind close-drawn blinds, cabarets and estaminets are full of revelling crowds. The natural, overflowing gaiety of a Frenchman cannot be checked by a mere War! There is a great deal to be said, after all, for the philosophy of "Eat, drink, and be merry"—at any rate, in France.

Oct. 27

King George V rode through Bailleul this morning, with the French President and the usual following of flunkeys and Staff Officers.

Oct. 31

The King is reported to have been seriously injured by a fall from his horse. He has been taken back to London.

   We are working now as Hospital Orderlies, which is the last job the Lord intended me for. However, we are lucky to have such cozy quarters. The real soldiers are doing men's work in the trenches, and we ought to be ashamed to look them in the eye.

Nov. 10

The Hospital was inspected today by General Alderson. Armentieres, for the past few days, has been subjected to a heavy bombardment. Bailleul, I believe is almost out of range.

Nov. 21

Paid a visit this afternoon to some Island boys in the C.M.R. [Canadian Mounted Rifles] (2nd Division). They are billeted just two miles up the road from town. Had a convivial evening.

December, 1915—London Leave and End of a Perfect Spree

Dec. 3   Bailleul.

I arrived back this morning after a nine-days' Leave to London. The journey, both ways, was a nerve-racking one. The Channel-crossing left me shaken with cold and seasickness. And London is not the gay town it was a year ago. Nevertheless, I spent a very good time, and would only too gladly go through it again. The theatres are all running to "Reviews" which do not interest me much. But I saw Dorris Kean in "Romance" and, at another house, "The Scarlet Pimpernel." I had a most enjoyable supper at "Ye Cheshire Cheese,"—a famous old Tavern on Fleet Street. Here it was that Dr. Johnson, Burke, Goldsmith, Sir Joshua Reynolds, and many other Eighteenth-century wits, were wont to gather. The old customs are kept up, as much as possible. For any lover of Boswell, the place is rich with associations, one can still call for a foaming pint of "'arf and 'arf," and ballast it with "corn beef" or "lark-and-kidney pie." The Port-Wine is something to sing about to the fourth and fifth generations. I encountered an old gentleman, in the Bar, who assured me that he had been drinking there "For nigh on seventy year." He still appeared quite thirsty. The Tavern is a great haunt for newspapermen.

The Temple Gardens, between Fleet Street and the Thames Embankment, drew my interest more than any other place in London. Half the literature of England must have been produced in this vicinity. Here, in Brick Court, is Goldsmith's house, where he "frittered away his time" writing "worthless poetry." He is buried here too, right behind the "Temple Church",—the Church of the old Crusaders. Irving, in his Sketch Book has a fine description of these Gardens. Dickens loved to haunt the place. I must not forget that it was here, according to Shakespeare, they plucked "the red rose and the white," in old time. Nor that, in Temple Hall, (still standing in perfect condition), the play of Twelfth Night was first produced, before Queen Elizabeth. I visited again Westminster Abbey, St. Paul's, British Museum, Art Gallery, etc.

The Golden Altar

A Knight I met, in a poet's tale,
  Penned of the days of the Simple Creed;
Who, riding in quest of the Holy Grail,
  Led once to a lonely Chapel his steed.

Therein he doff'd his helm and plate,
  His gilded spurs and his shield of fame;
And humbly there did he consecrate
  His sword, his life, to the one Great Aim.

The Chapel was silent, cold and bare,
  —What wondrous vision did he see;
All night long, on his knees in prayer,
  Keeping the Vigil of Chivalry?

What is he now, the valiant knight?
  Dust, with his crested arms uncouth,
But the fire that he kindled is burning bright
  On the altar shrined in the Heart of Youth.

Still on that altar, wrought of gold,
  His curious legends Time doth write;
And there enrolled are the warriors bold,
  Who ride to conquer themselves in fight.

Incense shall thro' the years uprise,
  Beacon to age and age the same;
For the jealous Spirit of Sacrifice
  Watches, and fans, and feeds the flame.

Dec. 25   Christmas Day—Bailleul.
Very little worth writing about, except it would be the turkey dinner we have just finished! Everybody happy.

January, 1916

Jan. 1   New Year's Day.
New Year's Day. Same as Christmas Day,—minus the dinner.

Jan. 31
The amusements in Bailleul are beginning to pall on us. When off duty, we find the time long enough. The only excitement is the occasional air raid. This morning, in the rue de Gare, women and children were killed in one of these raids. Bombs, dropped so unexpectedly from a clear sky, are more nerve-racking than a salvo of shells in a regular engagement.

Feb. 22
This morning the house-tops are covered with a mantle of snow,—the first I've seen since leaving Canada.

February, 1916—Trench Duty

Feb. 25   Dranoutre.
Moved at last, and nobody sorry! We were getting tired of the flesh-pots anyway, and a little bit of real active service is what we need. We are taking over from the 3rd Field Ambulance here, and will work in Stretcher-squads, as before, from the various Aid Posts.

Feb. 29
It is hard to sleep through the nightly racket of gunfire. German planes have been scouring about, overhead—like a flock of gaunt vultures,—all the morning. They symbolize Trouble.

Mar. 10 —Wulverghem. Advanced Dressing Station.
We relieved "B" Section this morning, and sent them cheerfully packing back along the Neuve Église Road.

The scenery about here is nothing much but shell-holes and heaps of debris. We are right on a hill. From the Dressing Station, it is possible to see Messines and the German lines.

The Soldier's Letter

Try as I will, dear one, 'tis hard to write
      Kind words of greeting, tender love, this day:
Such thoughts are all so very far away
As I would fain recall, for your delight!
The war has wrapped me in its own black night;
Hopeless and tired, I lack the strength to pray
So do not hush the children's noisy play
To speak of me, and cloud their faces bright.

Yet, in this pause before to-morrow's strife—
Even amid the dreariness of pain
Which makes death seem a kindlier thing than life,
One fancy I had lost comes back again:
Gratefully will the children's tears repay
In after years, what we have borne to-day!

March, 1916—A Quiet Line

Mar. 11   At the Aid Post of the 13th Battalion.

The Line is very quiet. It has rained a great deal lately, and the roads and trenches are flooded with water. We have been issued rubber hip-boots. The rats here are becoming altogether too familiar for comfort. Great lusty old fellows, hairless and tailless, run about all night, over bunks and floor and tables, squawking and squeaking. They gathered for a sort of Donnebook Fair, about two in the morning, and between them finished up all our bread rations.

Mar. 14

One of our Bearers—Fletcher—caught a stray bullet in the leg last night, coming down from the 13th Aid Post. This is our first casualty for a long time. The shell-fire sometimes gets bad, about the Dressing Station. But we have a good cellar.

Mar. 16   Aid Post of the 1st Battalion.

Business is rushing ... Officers are running down the Line, shouting for "Stretcher Bearers," and our whole Staff is turned out. There is a great deal of shell-fire, which makes carrying overland a ticklish job. At night it is even worse, on account of the stray bullets. One fellow told me that Wulverghem Road was haunted. It certainly is. It is haunted with the Shadow of Death.

Mar. 17

We "stood to" last night, expecting more German attacks. But the Line is quiet again. Yesterday's casualties amounted to some thirty wounded, seven dead. This was in the 1st Battalion only.

Mar. 18   Aid Post. 13th Battalion.

More excitement. This morning Fritz started shelling, in a careless, absent-minded sort of way. A "whiz-bang" ripped through the sheet-iron roofing of the Aid Post and exploded with a bang in the doorway. By some miracle of Providence, not a man was touched. Following this, the big-calibre shells began coming over. We scattered for the nearest Fire-trench. In an hour, all was clear again. Such incidents as this are not unusual, but they never fail to cause excitement; and they are the source of many long, hair-raising narratives, (in which the victims figure as the heroes)—told at bedtime, or over the beer-glass, or drafted with wonderful imaginary touches, into a

God's Acre: Ypres Salient
(On the Anniversary of April, 1915)

Statesmen or saint—when these are dead
     We raise the tomb, the statue head!
What for our own, our kindred bred,
Prodigal ones—
Slumbering in an alien bed
Dirged by the guns?

Did Folly lead, in milder days,
Blindly their steps from Virtue's ways?
Had youth, rash-blooded, scorned delays
When Passion willed?
Ah! but they met Death's baffled gaze
With courage filled.

Musing upon this hallowed plain
I hear once more the shrieks of pain,
I see the trenches, choked with slain
In Freedom's van,
A Remnant, charging on again,
To the last man.

No dogmas can the truth confound,
Each sodden patch of hard-won ground,
Each dingy cross, each rude-shaped mound,
—Their soldier-mead—
Proclaims a glory sought and found,
And stamps a creed.

...continued

Letter. We are all a great bunch of Boys out here, and nothing delights us more than to be allowed to strut a bit.

Mar. 24   13th Battalion Aid Post.
We were again shelled out this afternoon, and had to take to the knee-deep-with-mud Fire trench. The nights are very dark now, and "carrying out" is an arduous task. We have to pick our way by the light of the flares, over the wires and shell-holes. Stray bullets are the greatest source of danger.

Mar. 26   Dranoutre. Main Dressing Station.
We were relieved today by the 73rd (Territorial) Field Ambulance. The Canadian Division is being withdrawn from the trenches, for rest and re-enforcement.

Mar. 27   Poperinghe.
A year ago, before the memorable Battle of Ypres, we were marching over this very country, which had for us then all the charm of novelty. The guns have wrought little change since. The scared inhabitants, who last April were flying from home and business, are now back again, cheery as ever. Constant proximity to danger has made them callous of Death. Further up the Line,—quite within shell-fire,—it is a common sight to see them ploughing the fields, or cropping potatoes.

Apr. 7   Brandhoek.
Our gun-positions here are being shelled constantly, and every day the German planes are overhead. Close by our billet is a Regiment of Cold-stream Guards.

April, 1916—Ypres Once More
Apr. 11   Main Dressing Station Ypres.
Everything here is in a state of destruction impossible to describe. It is a city of the dead, and the present silence of the guns makes a stillness almost unearthly. At night, the flares from the trenches light up all the old skeletons of bygone grandeur—the Cloth Hall[4], the Cathedral, etc., and

---

4. Norm Christie, *For King & Empire* (Winnipeg: Bunker to Bunker Books, 1996), 5, talks about Ypres at its peak in the 13th century: At this time construction of the town's most famous building, the great Lakenhalle (Cloth Hall), a monument to Ypres' textile industry, was begun. Taking 100 years to build, this impressive covered market allowed ships to moor alongside to load and discharge cargoes onto a covered quay along the banks of the Yperlee.

...continued

Who might not bide, whate'er befall,
When the dread trumpet summons all
The mighty host—when Gabriel's call
Sounds God's Parade—
If he with them to stand or fall
Shall be arrayed!

burn into the soul of the observer a picture of woe that can never fade. The Cathedral alone is a tragedy. Broken and mutilated by the guns, the images of saints and apostles lie buried in every pile of debris. From the still-standing cross, protected by a fragment of wall, Christ gazes down.

Apr. 12   Advanced Dressing Station. Maple Copse.
After a long tramp over dirty roads and along a mile of communication trenches, we reach our new Dressing Post. We are in a small wood, hidden by ridges on three sides, about six hundred yards from the German lines. We have been issued the new steel shrapnel helmets.

Apr. 15
There is very little doing. We average about two stretcher trips a day. Bridge, Euchre, Cribbage, and Poker going strong. We are "breaking in" the advance party of the 9th Field Ambulance, who have freshly arrived. This is where the "long, hair-raising narratives" come in.

Apr. 21   Rest Billet. Reningelst.
We are very comfortable here, in a big, roomy hayloft. It's good to see unshelled fields and standing houses again.

April, 1916—Phillips Gets His
Apr. 27
The gun-positions here are always drawing shell-fire. We got a dose of it this morning, and Phillips, my old pal, has gone down the line badly wounded.

Apr. 30
We were roused from bed at one o'clock this morning by the Gas gongs. All along the line, the sirens and whistles and gongs were giving out their warning, and the guns were pounding away in apparently every direction. The flares were going up, red, white, and green, like Japanese fireworks.—It was almost worth the getting up, to see. But it was all a farce. They had been expecting Fritz to come over, and everybody had "the wind up."

May 1
Another Gas Alarm this morning—early. It was another farce, but it didn't strike us as being at all funny or interesting. We went back to bed in high dudgeon.

Arthur Phillips (Walker's best friend), Stretcher Bearer.
Wounded at Brandhoek on the Ypres-Poperinghe Road.

Warm weather is here again and outdoor life is a day-long picnic. We spend the most of our time playing ball, pitching quoits, etc. Our officers never bother us much with "Drill" when we are out of the Line, and our whole energies are thus thrown into sport.

The evenings can be very agreeably spent in Poperinghe, where hospitality and good cheer go hand in hand with all those feminine charms so dear to the heart of a soldier. *Honi savait.*

May, 1916 — On Working Party

May 13
Sent up to Kruisstraat last night on Working Party. We worked till daylight filling sandbags. This job aught to be part of the Kaiser's punishment, after the War. When I think of all the sandbags, from Ypres to the Somme, that have been filled so patiently and so painfully since 1914—! I cannot bear even to think on it!

May 19
More sandbags. We are building a new Dressing Station at Kruisstraat, which accounts for our labors. The Line is very quiet.

May 21   Reningelst.
Fire broke out at the Engineer's Dump here, and the ammunition supplies are catching it. Bombs and hand grenades are popping off by the hundreds.

June, 1916 — Third Battle of Ypres

June 6   "The Mill," Main Dressing Station, Vlamertinghe.
We are in the thick of a big battle now. Last Friday the Germans rushed our trenches at Lillebeck and Maple Copse, capturing ground, prisoners, and much ammunition and supplies. Trenches have been obliterated with shell-fire. Our Infantry are holding the Line from shell-holes. The Dressing Station here is crowded with wounded.

June 7   Advanced Dressing Station, "Railway Dug-Outs."
We arrived here—three stretcher squads of us—this afternoon. Along the Ypres road were scattered the debris of War—rifles, pieces of equipment, ammunition limbers, ration wagons, and dead horses. Guns of all calibre are massed hereabouts. The small guns are firing continuously. The Dress-

Stretcher bearers: Tom Horton, Montreal; Frank McManus, Saint John, NB.

ing Station is built into the Railway Embankment, and is practically shell-proof.

June 14

For forty-eight hours we have been working without a stop, and still the fighting is going on, and the wounded are falling faster than we can pick them up. It has rained all week. The trenches are knee-deep,—in some places waist-deep, with mud and water. The dead and wounded lie every-where: in trenches, and shell pits, and along the sodden roads. Two thousand wounded have passed through our hands since the attack. Hundreds more are dying of exposure a mile away, and we cannot reach them. The wounded who are already here must lie outside the Dressing Station, in the open, under the rain, until their turn comes.

We shall be relieved tonight, for twelve blessed hours, by the 3rd Field Ambulance. We are all in.

June 15

Wounded still coming in. The heavy fighting is over for the present.

June 16

Worked yesterday and last night up till 4 in the morning. We are now clearing German wounded. Many of them are in a horrible state of misery. With arms and legs off, they have been lying for days out in the rain. Their wounds have developed gangrene and blood poisoning, and very few of them will live to see Hospital. The gunfire has decreased to normal again.

June, 1916—Counter-Attacks

June 17

Last night, the Germans began counter-attacking. It should have been dark, but the whole Salient was ablaze with the gun-flashes and the sputtering, shooting star-shells. A shell might burst close by, and not make any impression on the senses, for it would never be heard above the racket of the guns. A Field Battery, behind our Dressing Station, caught a direct "hit." Up went the ammunition limber, and soon the whole pit was blazing. Starting up to "The Post."

Picket Thoughts

I saw God paint a rainbow in the sky,
    — And wondered why;
For even the while its freshness brought delight,
    It vanished quite!

I nursed a seedling tenderly to flower:
    It bloomed an hour.
It had proved my humble garden's pride
    — only it died.

Oh! I shall see that rainbow in the sky,
Portalled eternally above mine eye,
    Nor wonder why!
And I shall find the footpath to that valley,
Where the old songs and the old summers rally,
    And angels dally.

What if the star was gone
That led Columbus on, —
    Quenched in the void of night, ages before
    Were ghost-gleam from afar —
    He thought it still a star
Chartered a sea with it, and found new shore!

June 22   The Mill: Vlamertinghe.

We were relieved tonight by "C" Section.

June 30   Rest Camp—Whippenhoek Siding.

Cozy billets again. We have shower baths here, and many other unbeliev-
able luxuries. A few hundred yards away, along the Poperinghe Road, is
No. 3 Casualty Clearing Station—a brave display of well-trimmed lawn
and flower-beds, and huts brilliant in whitewash and fresh paint. They say
there are real nurses here, too.

Aug. 2

For the past two months, all Leave to England has been cancelled. The
offensive on the Somme Front is going steadily forward. We are still running the Rest Camp here,—a job that could not fail to satisfy the laziest
man on earth.

Aug. 9

The 1st Brigade is on the move today. We are packing up, ready for the
expected Order.

August, 1916—"For Fresh Fields and Pastures New"

Aug. 13

Sunday. Break camp this morning and follow the 2nd Brigade in Column
of Route. Bivouac for the night in open fields near Steenvoorde.

Aug. 14   On the Line of March.

The weather is beautifully fine and warm. Green fields and brown hedge-
rows lie all along the way. We bivouac for the night in open fields, "under
the wide and starry sky," as Stevenson would have it.

The 4th Canadian Division, freshly landed in France, is taking over
our old lines at Ypres.

Aug. 15

After another hot march of twenty kilometres, we pitch camp in wooded
fields near the village of Eperlecques.

Aug. 22

It rains at times, even in this fair part of the country; and as our "Camp"
consists of bivouacs, made from blankets and rubber sheets hitched to

hedges, we get the full benefit of whatever weather is going. Last night it poured down most dolefully, and all morning we have been drying out around the cook-fire.

The fine days are spent in arduous training. We have long marches every afternoon with "skeleton equipment." Sometimes the orders are "Route-march with full kit," and then we have to break up house and pack it along with the other junk. The Infantry Regiments are encamped about us, in fields and barn-billets. The whole is going through courses of stiff training.

Aug. 29   Candas

After a day's train-ride from Arques to Abbeville, and a long night march over muddy roads, through rain, we arrived at this little village. Pitched Bivys in open field. Everybody, (including Officers and the Sergeant Major!) had that pitiful, fed-up-and-far-from-home look, so peculiar to wet-weather pedestrians.

But this morning, with the sun shining and the birds chirping from the straw stooks, and the fresh country air blowing Réveillé in our faces, Life doesn't look too bad at all.

August, 1916—The March to the Somme

Aug. 30

All hands are washed, shaved and dried out now. The Sergeant Major is smiling again. Breaking camp early, we join up with the 2nd Brigade, and fall in on the Line of March.

(11 A.M.) Rain again. The Sergeant Major has quit smiling. For the remainder of the day it simply pours, and after making about sixteen kilometres through the puddles, we halt, pitch Camp, and crawl in for the evening, stripping ourselves to the skin and making a Christmas tree of the tent-poles, with our dripping clothes.

Sep. 1   Contay

The sun is out again, and we break camp this morning, proceeding cheerfully on our way, behind the Brigade. Arriving at the village of Contay, we take over Divisional Rest Billets from the 6th (Australian) Field Ambulance, who has been lined up about the old Chateau grounds, for hours, waiting our Relief.

September, 1916—We Reach Albert

Sep. 4   Main Dressing Station of the 3rd Field Ambulance, "North Chimney," Albert.

We have come up here, a half-dozen squads of us, to relieve No. 3. There is enormous traffic going on about Albert. Day and night through the streets go the long lines of cars—ambulance cars, munition cars, ration cars, limber cars, Staff cars. Thousands of troops are on the move through the city. One could imagine the whole British Army was in sight or hearing, so great is the impression left upon the mind by the ceaseless bustle and ordered confusion. Albert is flanked by long, sloping hills, upon which armies are encamped with guns and gun supplies. The Cathedral, which stands in the middle of the city, is much battered by shell-fire. The tall steeple was hit in the early days of the war and now hangs, from the centre downwards, over the street. The French peasants really believe the prophecy, that when this tottering steeple falls, the war will finish in victory.

"North Chimney"—where the Dressing Station is situated,—gets its name from a tall chimney over an old tumble-down machine shop, on which Father Time and the Germans have sported themselves. We are busy all night loading Ambulance Cars.

September, 1916—The Somme

Sep. 5   Advanced Dressing Station, Old German Dugouts, "Casualty Corner," on the "Chalk Pit Road," three kilometres beyond Albert.

We left Albert at 4:30 this morning with nine stretcher squads. The firing-line is two miles in front of us. A more drearily desolate piece of country could not be very well imagined. Here, a few short weeks ago, ran the German trenches. When the advance came, everything was left in wild disorder, for in the face of such terrible fire as our guns were putting up, nothing could stay and live. The muddy roads are strewn yet with broken-down cars and carts and limbers, and with unexploded shells and bombs, hidden in the debris—piles of discarded equipment. And it has been raining here for weeks. The shell holes and trenches are full of water, which probably hide many unguessable horrors, for there are thousands of unburied dead about here, and to go poking casually in a puddle you have a fifty-fifty chance of unearthing the arm, or leg, or skull of some body.

A hundred yards ahead of the Dressing Station is the village of Contalmaison—or what is left of it! Here it was that the Prussian Guards made their desperate stand,—a grim fight to the last man,—which cost England

"An Old Song Resung"

The gods have left Olympus, and their altar-stones are
      cold,
Their temples in the dust are lying low;
The plunder-laden chariots of their favored ones of old
Have crumbled into powder long ago.

The gods were great in ancient times (as brave old Homer
      sang)
When Greek and Trojan clashed in battle throes;—
Upon the windy plain of Troy—and loud their armor
      rang,
Like iron under Vulcan's hammer blows.

The Trojans battled bravely with their javelins and
      shards;
They swept the field, with Hector in the van;
But they hadn't a real chance to win—the gods had
      stacked the cards,
And marked them out for slaughter, every man.

But though they went to slaughter, boys, I don't believe
      they're dead!
They shed their skins to give their souls more ease.
The fighting soldier never dies (as brave old Homer said)
He goes on marching down the centuries.

And Hector may be here to-day wherever the Khaki fits!
And any old song's a marching song of Troy
As we swing good Canadian legs beneath our dusty
      Kits—
And hark the little Yankee drummer-boy!

On the line of March 1916

dear. Bravery it was, too! But we have no time for even the common decencies now, and these, the Flower and pride of the German Army, are left to rot unburied on the field.

The Dressing Station is in a deep dug-out, most luxuriously fitted out. It was probably the Headquarters of a German Regiment and some of the boys have been digging up officers' helmets, uniforms, revolvers, etc.

September, 1916—Battle of Pozières Wood—The Somme
Sep. 6   Aid Post of the 8th Battalion.
Worked till noon under heavy shell-fire. Captain Jeff, the officer in charge of Squads, and two Bearers, wounded. We must carry here "across country" for the narrow trenches are filled with Infantry re-enforcements. From the Aid Post, we are in plain view of the German lines, and all the squads carry white flags for protection. We could see German stretcher-squads working on the other side. The country is all mud and barbed-wire, and the shell holes are so crowded that they elbow one another. Some of them are quite deep enough to drown a man, when full of water,—as they often are. The Australians told us at Contay that we were going into no "boys' job." They should have used stronger language than that!

We were relieved this afternoon by "No. 3," and will be off-duty for twenty-four hours.

Sep. 9
We are working in regular shifts, twenty-four hours on, twenty-fours off,—and have had no further casualties. On both sides the Artillery fire is constant, but what had appeared to us, on our arrival here, as the sights and sounds of big battle, proves only to be the usual everyday "straaf,"—the regular thing which has been going on for months.

September, 1916—The Somme—An Air Battle
Sep. 11
The aeroplane activity alone, every day, would be quite enough to make life interesting out here. No grander tournaments were ever staged in the old days of Chivalry, than what these 20th-century knights pull off so nonchalantly in the blue sky. This morning saw a grand duel between a British and a German squadron of planes. They battled up there in the clouds for some thirty minutes, to the immense satisfaction of the scattered audience below which, to the number of some quarter-million, cheering lustily

From the Somme

I

Just as the sun sinks behind the sombre brooding trees
Ere yet the sentry-stars their customed watch have ta'en,
Weary with the world's woe—amid the great guns'
      blasphemies—
Christ leads the stretcher-squads over the Fields of Pain.

II

Death came savagely here, swift in the night
Leaving a Song unsung, a Tale untold—
Leaving only this in the blanket-fold,
To be buried darkly away, where rats won't bite;—
Leaving only a Cross scratched with a stone
To carry all Life's Poem and History;—
"Number and name and Regiment, unknown;
Fell on the field of Battle. R. I. P."

Courcelette (on the Somme)
1916

from every corner of the Line. The fight centred around two machines, which were manoeuvring about each other like hostile eagles. Backwards and forwards, over the breathless trench-lines they soared, each seeking to swoop upon the other from higher ground. Finally, "our man" got the advantage, opened his deadly machine-gun fire, and sent his opponent blazing to the ground, where he landed with the sickening thud of a thunderbolt—like Milton's angel—"Hurled headlong flaming from the ethereal sky."

During the fight, all traffic had halted and the whole activity of War seemed to have stopped like a piece of clock-work. Now the wheels automatically started again—teams trudged over the roads as before; men picked up their discarded rifles, or fell into step, or went back to dinners and card-games; and the Colonels climbed back into their dug-outs.

The Somme—The Tanks Arrive—The Battle of Courcelette

Sept. 20 "Casualty Corner"

We have just returned from Contay, where we were sent for two days rest-up. Even while off duty here, it is hard to sleep with the racket the guns are making, and the dug-outs are crawling with rats and vermin.

The 2nd and 3rd Divisions have been doing hard fighting lately, and our Line is advanced now beyond Courcelette and Martinpuich. In these last battles, we have been using a new and terrible-looking engine of War,—land-ships, or "Tanks," as they are officially called. These monster things are like great armoured cars on caterpillar wheels, which will carry them over any obstacle. They roll about in a cumbrous, unconcerned way over barbed wire, shell-holes, trenches, anything. An Infantryman told me it was the funniest thing he ever saw,—the tanks strolling over Fritz's Front Line and crushing gun-emplacements like eggshells. I thought he had rather a strained sense of humor; but no doubt they look funny enough to anyone save the fellows ahead.

The three Field Ambulances of the 1st Division are now working together, and the Stretcher Bearers are running the "eight-hour shift" system, which gives us lots of rest. This, of course, can only be done between the heavier fighting. The "carry" from the Aid Post, at the "Sugar Refinery," is along the Maple Leaf Road, and this road is literally flooded. Road, trenches, shell-holes,—all look alike, and at night it is arduous work to keep one's footing in the mud. To carry a mile along this road in the dark is a good two hours' job. We have instituted "Relay Posts" along the Road, so as to facilitate the work.

Home!

Sandy shores, and dusty roads that wander town-
      wards from the sea.
Up-and-down, and up-and-down, and up-and-down
      again,
Pasture lands and berry lands, where spruce and tangled
      hawthorn be;
Clover fields, and barley fields, and fields of sunning
      grain!

Big brown men in over-alls, who nod a friendly "How
      d'ye do?"
And halt their teams, and ask your way, and pick
      you up with care;
White-walled cotts, and open doors where hunger-
      'peasing smells come through,
Weary traveller does not ask his plaintive question there!

The Somme—Resting Up

Sep. 26   Main Dressing Station. Albert.

How good it is to get into semi-civilization again! To see houses and chickens and children once more, after the hermit isolation of trench life! The old woman with the harelip, even, in the Estaminet at Contay would "look good" to us now! How pleasant it is to have been dog-tired, and wet through, and weary, and then to come back to hot baths and warm beds again!—and to wake up, after eighteen hours sleep, to beans and bacon! and to light cigarettes and smoke and read and sleep and smoke again throughout another easy day!—and to have the Sergeant Major and the Sergeants and the other fellows who haven't been "Up the Line" so humbly civil to you!—and, last and best of all, to con over and over again the half-dozen letters from Home that have been waiting your return! This,—this is true felicity. These are perfect hours, snatched from the hand of "envious and culminating Time."

The Somme—We Get Hit Hard

Sep. 30   Advanced Dressing Station Pozières Wood.

We have been working like niggers for the past two days, along with the other Ambulance men, and everybody else we could coax or bully into helping us. On the morning of the 27th, a real fight developed, and we are busy yet clearing out the Aid Posts. The Germans are keeping up heavy barrage-fires behind the Lines, which make our work a series of Marathon races from Post to Dressing Station. Among the Bearers, we have already had some twenty casualties. McNutt, Lacey, Bill Woods, Joe McDonald,—all my best pals,—are gone down wounded. McNutt has been hit through the back, and has very little chance. His squad was carrying right ahead of us when the fatal shell came over. It burst full upon them, scattering them like nine-pins, and a crazy sort of laughter came from our lips when we saw the Patient leap from the abandoned stretcher and go tearing across country for the nearest trench. McNutt also jumped and ran for the trench, with the others. We rushed on with our own case as best we could, and reported the trouble at the Dressing Station. Mac has gone down the Line in a special car. "Drive like hell!" said the Major. But he won't live.

The Dear Days
(A Reminiscence)

If I could rub Aladdin's Lamp,
     And bring the Genie to my call,
I'd bid him fetch from Time's cold hand
     The hours I cherish most of all:
I'd have the days brought back again
We tented on the English plain!

O days of Hardship and Romance,
     When, shivering through the wintry weather,
Beneath the dripping cheese-cloth tents,
     We lived, and laughed, and sang together!
Those days upon the wind-swept plain
     Are dearer for the mud and rain.

The songs we'd sing by brazier-light!
     How roared the chorus round the line
Of "Fare thee well, my own True Love!"
     And "O, my darling Clementine!"
And "A fond kiss and we must sever!"
And "Dixie Land," and "Swanee River!"

The talks we'd have when lights were out,
     The camp all silent on the hill!
Jim loved the best girl ever was:
     And so did I; and so did Bill!
We'd whisper this and that and t'other,
     Baring our hearts to one another.

...continued

The Somme
Oct. 1   Hérissart.
A small, sleepy village, fifteen kilometres behind the Line. We are back now for rest and re-enforcements. Life seems dead now, with so many of the old boys gone! Everyone is affected, more or less, by the absence of these familiar faces in the morning Parade. Like old home-teams, that have worked well and long together, we cannot accommodate ourselves to these new fellows that have been thrust upon us by accident and adversity.

Oct. 6   Albert.
We have moved to billets here, and will be kept in readiness for any trouble. The Unit is quite up to strength again, as far as numbers are concerned. McNutt has died at Amiens hospital. He was game right to the end, they say. It would be hard to find a nobler death than that of a Stretcher Bearer, and in Mac's case it has been well-earned.[5]

"Regina Trench"
Oct. 8   Advanced Post. Courcelette.
Today was one of general confusion. The 3rd Brigade attacked in the morning and gained "Regina Trench," but owing to poor support and shortage of bombs, lost it again, along with a considerable number of men. We started for Courcelette in Stretcher squads after the initial attack, tramping along the muddy Pozières Road. The shell-fire was very heavy, as we approached the ridge of the little hill which ran into the town, and we were forced to abandon the road and take to the communication trenches. These trenches were spreading out every hundred yards in half a dozen directions, and as we had no idea of the lay of the country, and could not keep our heads long above the ground to find it out, we eventually lost our way. Bill Grover and I turned back and made for Pozières again, where we took to the old road, and (as the shelling had somewhat abated) followed it into Courcelette. But not without an exciting experience on the way. For just as we had started, we saw, above us climbing the ridge, an ambulance wagon. And as it approached the summit a shell came over, killing two of the horses. The driver unhitched the remaining team, and beat it, leaving the wagon, with its freight of wounded, alone on the hill. It was really the only thing he could do. Then, as we drew towards the top, another wagon

---

5. Editor's Note: One further sentence, deleted by Dad, basically says that he and Mac had often "talked over the chances."

...continued

The sprees we'd have when pay day came!
    What jolly tramps to Salisbury Town!
(With a short, sweet halt at the Bustard Inn
    Where the ale was always a good nut-brown)
Sometimes we'd tow Jim back again—
    Ah me, those days upon the Plain!

How few are left for laughter and song!
    Bill don't sing much back home, I bet;
And poor old Jim, he's silent now
    Behind a trench, near Courcelette;
And me, I'm sticking at the game
Out here; but life don't seem the same.

team came, and another shell was fired. We were quite near to the ridge now, and we could see the canvas top of the ambulance shaking back and forth as the driver lashed the horses and clung to his seat. Two more shells were fired, and the cumbrous, rumbling wagon rocked in the concussion, but still the driver kept his seat, and still the horses plunged on,—on over the top, and safely down the other side. We cheered, Bill and I,—though the excited driver never heard us, or even noticed us, as he drove madly by. It was like watching a movie show. But now we had to take the ridge ourselves. We shut our teeth and sprinted. Nothing happened. We felt a little cheap. Fritz would not be bothered wasting a shell on us, of course, and as he could see the ridge plainly, he must have enjoyed our exhibition of speed. We reached the Aid Post without further mishap, and secured a drink of Rum.

It is dark now, and the Aid Post is full of wounded. Stretcher cases are lined outside along the trenches, and many will be left there for hours.

The Somme
Oct. 10   Old Dug-Outs. La Boiselle.
We got down here somehow—God only knows how!—for a brief rest. It is the first for two days. Rum and the excitement was all that kept us going. The wounded are about cleared up—though there are some yet in over-looked places. We have had some more casualties among the Bearers. One of the late re-enforcements was blown to pieces a few hundred yards from the Aid Post.

Oct. 12   Courcelette.
We are working again in the old twenty-four shifts. The Line is quiet. The only cases worth mentioning are those terrible ones which have been lying out for days in No Man's Land. Their condition is truly pitiful. In many cases, merciful death has come, but where slight wounds have turned to gangrene and fever, there is nothing to be done but make them as comfortable as possible. We bear them back to safety, but I often think that a quick bullet would be the kinder mercy.

Oct. 14
Henry, our Section Sergeant, was badly wounded coming in tonight. He jumped for a trench to avoid the fragments of a bursting shell, and impaled himself upon a bayonetted rifle which had been left carelessly, upright in the ground. The bayonet, which was a dull and rusty one, penetrated some three inches into the groin. We carried him back.

Aftermath

With Desolation and the Stars
      I lonely vigil keep,
Over the garner'd fields of Mars,
      Watching the dead men sleep—
            Huddled together, so silent there.
            With bloodless faces and clotted hair,
      Wrapped in their long, long sleep!

By uptorn trees and crater rims
      Along the Ridge they lie,
Sprawled in the mud, with out-spread limbs,
      Wide staring at the sky.
            Why to the sky do they always stare,
            Questioning heaven in dumb despair?
Why don't they moan, or sigh?

Why do I rave, 'neath the callous stars,
      At their upturned faces white?
I, surely I, with my crimson scars
      Slumber with them this night!
            Death, with shadowy finger bare,
            Beckons me on to—I know not where;
            But, huddled together, and freed from care
      We'll watch till the dawn of Light.

From the Somme,
    1916

Relieved At Last

Oct. 15   Rest Billets. Albert.

We were relieved this afternoon by the 12th and 13th Field Ambulances. All hands are sick and tired and fed up. The whole Division is moving out now, with what remnants of Regiments are left. And if there's any more fighting to be done on the Somme, they'd better get someone else to do it.

We Leave The Somme

Oct. 17   On the Line of March.

We left Albert this afternoon, following up the 2nd Brigade. Camped for the night in open fields.

Oct. 18   Val De Maison.

These little villages are so much alike that to have seen one or two is to have travelled Northern France. — Straggling cobbled streets, flanked by red-tiled houses of all the odd shapes known, with here and there a pump-handle sticking out where the letter-box ought to be, — this is the general plan of them all. Then, of course, there is the "Grande Place" and the Cathedral, and the two or three corner Estaminets without which a French-man would never be at home.

We are billeted with some Gendarmes in a large brick out-building adjoining an even larger manure-pile, from whence every morning comes "the cock's shrill clarion" and the contented grunting of many pigs. We are getting back to nature.

Oct. 20   On the Line of March.

The weather is keeping fine just now. The complete exhaustion of the men is plainly seen in the numbers who are falling out of the march. We pick these stragglers up—all along the way, in our cars, as we follow behind the Brigade.

Oct. 22   On the Line of March.

The country side is rough and picturesque, stretching out in great waves like the swell of a sea. Ridges are dotted with grey mills and red cottages: the valleys are thickly wooded. We seem always to be climbing hills.

Oct. 23   On the Line of March.

We find a cozy billet tonight in the rooms of a Chateau, —a very aristocratic old place, sheltered amid great clumps of chestnut trees and surrounded

The Old Château

We halted once at an old Château;—
  —Tramping it back through the mud and rain,
  Dodging the traffic to and fro,
  And tickled to death to get out again:
We were glad to see God's green fields once more,
Glad to forget the guns' mad roar,
And we slept like babes on the damp, stone floor
  Of that old Château.

The old Château is a débris pile:—
  Mouldering sand-bags, broken glass,
  Fallen timber, and stone, and tile;
  And the garden is naught but graves and grass.
Great gaunt rats through the chambers leap,
Rank weeds over the flower beds creep—
'Tis a picture to make the angels weep,
  Is that old Château!

Generous days had the mansion known,
  Glorious nights of feast and song;
  Echoes of merry laughter flown
  Haunt it yet, and will linger long.
But for all the guests that throng'd its halls,
At parties, and banquets, and fancy balls,
Most grateful were we to the friendly walls
  Of that old Château.

by brick and stone fence-work of a burglar-proof pattern. The village of La Thienloye lies but a stone's throw away, and the second Estaminet on the right, I might add, has some very good wine for sale. We can get champagne, too, at five francs, but it is of the old familiar crabapple brew,—not worth drinking.

Oct. 27   Divisional Rest Camp. Grand Servins.

We take over new duties this morning, relieving the 73rd (Imperial) Field Ambulance. The Camp consists of the usual number of green army huts, artistically surrounded with grassy walks and whitewashed flower pots.

November, 1916—"Over the Beer Glass"

Nov. 30   Grand Servins.

The Infantry Battalions are being slowly brought up to strength again, re-enforcements are passing through the village constantly, and the memory of those six hard weeks on the Somme is falling back into the limbo of the past.

We have just drawn our extra Christmas pay (fifty francs) and the Estaminets have opened up for the evening. Cheery little Estaminet! How genial is your atmosphere, how hospitably open your doors to the weary step of the soldier! Here, over the cool bubbling beer glass, can be refought all the old battles, resung the old songs.

Amid the tinkling of the glasses and the laughter of Mademoiselle, and the inevitable jingling of the music-box (which plays the Marseillaise for the insertion of a penny in the slot)—how easily amid such sounds and scenes does the heart expand, the eye brighten, the cheek glow with animation. These are real hours of Life,—hours that will be lovingly recalled, in all their bright tints and colors, hours that sweeten the soul.[6]

Dec. 19   Bruay.

Bruay is a straggling dirty mining town of some thirty thousand population. But for the few larger stores, the houses and streets are all built alike—I don't know how the inhabitants find their way about at night, unless by some sixth sense of direction.

---

6. Editor's Note: One paragraph, deleted by Dad, speaks of how easy it is, amid such sounds and scenes, to "forget the dark shadow that is hanging over us all."

Our Sergeant

Our Sergeant, he's the veteran type the
    soldiers love the best;
He doesn't shine his Brass nor wear
    his Ribbons on his chest.
He's never laid a Gun, nor fired a shot,
    nor threw a Bomb,
But he knows the British Battle-front
    from Ypres to the Somme.

He thrives on Iron Rations, and he
    takes his Licker raw;
He's got the healthy organs of a mule
    from Arkansas;
The rumble of his voice has shook
    defaulters to the soul,
And the Sergeant-Major envies him
    —the way he bawls the Roll.

He'd led a rough and roving life
    before the War began;
Swinging an axe in lumber camps,
    driving a brewery van,
Digging Boston sub-ways, climbing
    telegraph poles in Maine
And always when his Luck was out
    he'd hit the Woods, again.

...continued

We are billeted, ten of us, with a miner's family. Our room is in the attic, and far from comfortable in this weather. The cook-house is a quarter-mile away, through slush-puddles.

Dec. 25   Christmas Day
Everybody broke. I've been hanging about the windy old attic all morning, shivering over a borrowed copy of *Childe Harold* and trying hard to forget it was my Birthday. We'll have a turkey dinner, I hope.

January, 1917—Broke in Bruay

Jan. 1
We're still broke. There is nothing much to write about. The weather keeps cold and miserable—our attic is about as cozy as a snowed up hen-coop. The wind blows dirges through the shivering rafters, and the rain beats time with solemn insistence upon the sodden floor. I tried to borrow a franc from the Sergeant this morning, but he had only ten-pence-half-penny, and it seemed a shame to take it. The Pay Master is discreetly keeping himself out of sight.

Jan. 9
Religion seems to be at a discount in Bruay. Nobody goes to church,—in fact, there isn't any church here. They profess to be Aetheists, or Agnostics, or some other thing of this sort. The shape of their heads doesn't give me any deep impression of superior mental vision. Why there should be communities of Aetheists in a country so professedly religious, is a curious thing.

The miners, many of them, have spent years in English or American collieries, and they speak English quite as well as the average Scotchman.

Jan. 11
Germans raided the aerodrome here this morning, causing much destruction but few casualties. Bombs are horrible things when they land in towns of this size,—among so many women and children.

...continued

Nature had given him length of limb,
    and a broad and powerful back;
He took to Stretcher-Bearing like
    a peddler to his pack;
He works his Squads like galley-slaves,
    whenever the job is grim,
And there's many a man in "Blighty" now
    who owes his luck to him. .

Rough and ready, strong and steady,
    manly all the while;
He's the kind the kings delight to
    honor with their smile!
Kings may come, and kings may go,
    Along the Battle Line
But he'll be "packing" stretchers
    til the end of bloody time.

The Great Man Looks at Us

Jan. 16   Bruay.

We were inspected today by General Currie, Canadian Commander. After standing up to the raw wintry wind on the market square for two hours, with full packs on, we eventually had the gratification of seeing this great man. The fact that he had kept us waiting so long did not, of course, worry him.

Jan. 21   Hirson.

The 2nd Divisional Ambulance has taken over our billets in Bruay—good luck to them! We are now in charge of the Rest Camp, stationed in a fine old chateau.

January, 1917— Cozy Billets

Jan. 28   Fosse 9 (Near Barlin).

The crowded Hospital quarters here are not sufficient for housing the Personnel, so we have been assigned our billets among the civilian population. The people are most hospitable and friendly. They treat us to everything in the house—and the cellar.

We are rooming with a family of Refugees who had lost all their earthly treasures in the early days of the War, when Lens was first captured by the Hun.

The old man works in the mine; the old lady and daughter keep house. Albert Dupuis (one of our garrulous French Canadians) has already fallen in love with the daughter, and they sit about every evening in the kitchen, cooing together like turtle doves, to the great disgust of the rest of us who (and he knows it) can't talk enough French to disturb his smirking complacency. But we all dine together, when the old man comes home from work, and then the family bosom widens to receive us.

Feb. 14

We were inspected today at Barlin by Field Marshall Sir Douglas Haig. He is, for his inches, the finest-looking soldier in the British Army. His inspection was very rapid. He walked briskly down the files, looking every man in the eye and holding his head cocked slightly to one side like a contemplative rooster,—his spurs, perhaps, strengthened this illusion.

FLANDERS FROM A STRETCHER-HANDLE

WAR RHYMES
BY
PRIVATE FRANK WALKER,
Field Ambulance,
1st Canadian Contingent.

In Loving Memory
OF
COMRADES WHO SLEEP
IN
FLANDERS' FIELDS.

FOLKESTONE:
ARTHUR STACE & SONS, 17 GRACE HILL.
1918.

February, 1917—Dug-Outs Again
February 28   Dug-Outs. Ariane Dump, in the vicinity of Neuville St. Vaast.

The Line is very quiet here. We are some two miles behind the trenches. In the background rises the battered church spire of Mont-St. Eloi, ahead are the tangled fields of barbed wire. Beside the dug-outs, running parallel with the trench lines, is the great Arras-Bethune high road—the road of the "Three Musketeers," where D'Artagnan galloped so bravely. It looks dismal enough now, for all its romantic memories. The spare fringe of lonely poplar trees that line it wave to and fro like uneasy ghosts. And Death walks this road at all hours. We have been busy fitting up a Dressing Station here, at the crossroads, in a deep, shell-proof dug-out which will hold some twenty stretcher cases.

March, 1917—Getting Ready For More Trouble
Mar. 8   Quatre Vents.

This patch of little Siberia is called "quatre vents" in French, or "the four winds." It is a little hamlet built about the road crossing, and quite fulfils its breezy title. We are busy erecting huts and marquee tents, in preparation for something which looks all too much like trouble.

April, 1917—The Battle of Vimy Ridge
Apr. 8   Ariane Dump. New Dressing Station.

All the Bearers have been sent up the Line tonight, to be in readiness for the expected Dawn-attack. The Line is ominously quiet.

Apr. 9   At the 5th Battalion Aid Post.

(11 A.M.) After an early breakfast this morning, we started working—the attack came off all right, and the struggling lines of wounded have been arriving now for hours. We met with a convoy of German prisoners coming down, and the Infantrymen in charge handed them over to us, for we needed more Bearers. We are using them now in squads. They show a natural impulse to carry out their own men first,—but we're bossing the job.

(7 P.M.) The German fire has died down completely. A great number of their guns have been taken or put out of action. The whole of Vimy Ridge is ours now, they say, and the 1st Division has crossed the railway lines at Willerval. Our Aid Post this evening is lying where the German

W.W. I. April, 1917

Packing Out
(A Ballad of the Stretcher Bearers)

I
We loaf around the Aid Post, on the sand bags in the
    sun,
Taking the jeers and sneers of every passing son-of-a-
    gun.
We are the lousy stretcher-squads, the discards of the
    Pack,
The idlers of the Army—til the Army's next attack!

II
And then, some bloody morning, when the sky's a
    blazing red,
And the batteries are roaring loud enough to wake the
    dead,
And the little mad machine-guns the infernal racket
    swell
With the din of devils riveting the boiler plates of hell.

III
—Oh, then it's "Good Old Stretcher-Bearers: they're the
    boys for trouble!"
"Gangway for the Stretcher-Bearers coming on the
    double!"
"Gangway for the Bearers!" goes from trench to trench
    the cry,
And everybody hops aside to let the "Bearers" by.

...continued

second-line trenches were—yesterday. We have to carry across the old No
Man's Land and this, in many places, is impossible. There are a great many
dead in the shell holes and many more, I suppose, buried amid debris
and dug-outs. We have been working steadily since morning. The Rum
Issue is short—one of the officer's "Batmen" stole a jugful, leaving us—the
Stretcher Bearers—to go bring.

April, 1917—Battle of Vimy Ridge
Apr. 10   Aid Post. "Nine Elms." Behind Farbus Wood.
The awful effects of our gunfire is apparent everywhere in the almost obliterated lines of trenches and dug-outs. It is no wonder Fritz "retired." He is
still on the run, in some places, and it is reported that Canadian Cavalry
have been in action.

The prisoners are dazed looking, unshaven, and dishevelled. They realize their own good fortune in being taken, however, and it would require a
machine gun squad to drive them back to their own lines again.

At Ariane Dump—so ominously quiet a few days ago,—the rumbling
of big lorries and limbers along the road is continuous. Railway lines are
being rapidly set across country, to communicate with our new trench-
lines. Everything is in a state of bustle and confusion.

April, 1917—Vimy Ridge
Apr. 15   "Nine Elms."
For the past few days, the newly won ground has been the scene of Titanic
labors. Roads of corduroy and steel rails are being run over the old "No
Man's Land"; salvage-squads are busy levelling the ground and clearing
away the battle debris. We can now move the wounded from the Aid Post
here right through to Ariane Dump on the small Railway, which saves us
enormous labor. Beyond the "Nine Elms," we must carry, from Willerval
and Farbus Wood, a distance of two kilometres.

It is reported that our total bag of prisoners, since the 9th, is over thir-
teen thousand, including a captured Brigadier General and his Staff.
Apr. 21
The Front has quieted down again to normal and, except for our own batteries, which are always barking, one might imagine that an Armistice was
on.

The weather has cleared: sun and wind are drying up the sodden battle
field. It is expected the Advance will be continued in a few days.

...continued

IV

Into the red confusion then, and through the din we
    pass,—
Stumbling along the trench mats, holding our breath for
    Gas—
Scrambling over the bald-spots, hearing the bullets
    whine—
Over the gaps and through the saps and up the Firing
    Line.

V

We go where men are falling in the awesome barrage-
    tract,
We dig them out, and pick them up, and pack them
    safely back.
Over the wire and through the mire and down the Line
    we go,
And you can bet your old Tin Hat our pace is far from
    slow!

VI

Back and back we go, til the battle-field is clear,
(It's good to hear the wounded chaps giving us the
    Cheer!)
Back and back we go til the bloody job is through,—
Then it's "Good old Stretcher Bearers!" and "A double
    Rum for you!"

Apr. 25   Farbus Wood.

From the wooded ridge which slopes steeply down towards Willerval, a grand view can be had of the battle front. The battered ruins of the villages of Willerval, Farbus, and Bailleul sprawl upon the plain below, and in advance of them is Arleux. Between Arleux and Willerval lie the opposing armies—but nothing is visible save ruins and shell holes, and battered trench lines, and barbed wire. Just now can be descried the smoke of our own shells, bursting over Arleux and, though this is quite three kilometres away, it seems much nearer. Indeed, our guns are giving the enemy no rest by day or night. Driven desperate, time and time again they have counter-attacked,—only to be mown down with machine gun fire. The game seems to be entirely in our hands,—we rest when we please, we attack when we are ready, and when we cease again, the Germans are only too pleased to follow suit. I am forgetting the aeroplane activity—there the Germans are supremely in command, for the time being. They have driven a number of our best men to the ground within the last few days.

One of our stretcher squads was actually chased by a German plane. He swooped upon them, (as they were climbing Farbus Wood), firing his machine gun and making them scatter for shell-holes until he spied our own planes coming along. These he easily eluded, and soaring heavenward in great spiry circles, retired to his own side of the Line.

April, 1917—I Visit Arras

Apr. 26   Arras.

Curiosity has driven me hither. As I am off duty for twenty-four hours,—and as this historic city lies so near, I thought it well worth a visit. But there is little to be seen, except ruins. The Cathedral, the Hotel de Ville, etc.—all are gone beyond redemption. The few civilians who remain here live in cellars and bomb-proof shelters, underground, like a great family of rats who must scatter frightened to their holes a dozen times a day. Pale faces and sunken eyes tell of many anxious days and nights spent in their Purgatory.

April, 1917—Attacks and Counter-Attacks

Apr. 28   Aid Post. Willerval.

We staged another successful attack this morning: and the 2nd Brigade, as a result, is now holding Arleux. Our heavy firing completely silenced the enemy's guns, and the Infantry walked into the old German lines without

We Who Return

We who return will understand,
      Cherish the glory of our Land;
Will call her dearer, love her more
Than ever she was loved before.
We who have tramped her outposts, kept
Our watches well; and have not slept!
We will return with vision clear,
Hands disciplined by duties done,
Demanding, as a Right we've won,
Proudly her chartered course to steer.

any trouble. The prisoners taken are mostly Prussians, and some of them are wearing, on their uniforms, a blue sleeve-band with the word "Gibraltar." This, indeed, was the identical Regiment that fought with the British against Spain in "Ye goode olde Dayes" when Gas or Machine-guns were never dreamed of, and when a man had to fight for about twenty years before he was considered a "veteran." For all their old alliances with us, the Prussians are the most desperately dangerous foe the British have to contend with. Unlike the "Saxons" or "Württembergers," they never crack jokes over the trenches. The "Gibraltar" patches are fast disappearing into Canadian pockets,—they make good souvenirs; and Prussia won't need them anymore.

Apr. 30   Willerval.

The Germans counter-attacked last night, in a vain attempt to recapture Arleux. They were driven back by our machine gun fire. Imperial troops on our right have captured Oppy, and fierce and continuous fighting can be heard in that direction. We are kept fairly busy, with the wounded, as the "carry" is long and arduous; but not dangerous.

May 1   Relay Post. Farbus Wood.

The Germans counter-attacked suddenly this evening—just at dusk. All along the line blazed our distress signals, in great shooting balls of fire and, instantly from behind us, opened up the guns. It was a glorious sight! In a few minutes, the whole line was brilliant with rockets and star-shells. Green, blue, red and white, they illuminated the sky for miles, in shooting sputtering loops of light, while the thundering guns blazed through the darker distance with their great belching mouths.

> "Like the fiery eyes of demons
> Fierce within their blinking lashes."

(Later) The attack has subsided. Fritz is silent now, and I guess his Stretcher Bearers are working their legs off—poor chaps.

May, 1917—Desperate Attacks

May 3   Aid Post of the 4th Batallion; in a sunken Road beyond Willerval.

Heavy fighting has been going on all morning. Fresnoy has been carried,—lost,—and carried again. The Germans are suffering heavy casualties, and our bag of prisoners is growing. These prisoners we are using as Stretcher Bearers. A Staff Officer captured admits that the best soldiers of the German

The Old Battle Field

Each has his grave among the many graves
    Planted in rich rows on the battle-field,
      Where, for a time, guns roared and columns
        wheeled
And now whereon the crimson poppy waves.
There the first robin comes, with piping staves,
    To sing of Summer all the long day through,—
    Over and over there, as if he knew
His were the ditties dear to the buried Braves.
And all around the graves, where these lie sleeping,
Seed-time and Harvest come, and men come reaping—
    Reaping the old grim field of strife and pain!
    Where the long tortuous lines of trench were
      drawn,
Where gas-clouds rolled, and shrapnel fell like rain,
And men walked, glory-crowned, to death, at Dawn.

Charlottetown, 1920

Army,— viz. The Prussian Guards, are in front of us, and that they have been ordered at all costs to hold the line.

(Later) We are still holding Fresnoy, and the English troops on the right are gaining ground. Gun fire is constant on both sides, but we are giving them two to one.

Arleux, which lies directly ahead of our Aid Post here, had been evacuated by the Germans a few days ago, and there remains there all kinds of stores, ammunition, equipment, food, wine, beer, tobacco, etc.—if one only knew where to find it, or had the time or inclination to look for it. At present, we have got our hands full.

May–July, 1917—We Recuperate
Jul. 22   Rest Billets. Fosse 9.

After many minor adventures and wanderings, during two months-and-a-half (of which I have kept no record), we find ourselves "back in the Family Bosom." The dear old lady is kissing all hands,—so pleased she is to see us safe again, and the daughter, I suppose, is kissing Dupuis in the kitchen. We were paid this afternoon, and life appears in all the rosy tints of youth and opulence. The boys will be painting the old town red tonight, and the officers will be looking the other way, for even the Sergeant Major will be content to let things slide for a while. We have been given great praise for our work in the Line, and the Colonel is as pleased as punch. He tried some troublesome "cases" this morning, and dismissed them. This is the best time to get into trouble,—when everyone is in such high humor!

Rambling Notes

My war journal has come to an end—I grew tired of making notes on every trivial occasion, and the novelty of writing about Active Service can no longer inspire my efforts. But the rest can be told very simply. After the battle of Passchendaele, I was invalided back to England, and for many months remained at Hospitals and Casualty-Depots there. I had Leave on several occasions, and visited many places of interest. In Scotland, I saw Glasgow, Edinburgh, and the Burns country around Ayr. I made a pilgrimage to Loch Lomond. I visited Canterbury and Carlisle, London, Liverpool, and Manchester. But old historic scenes, or great bustling cities had now lost much of their charm and interest. Where are all the merry, carefree crew, that made the old training days a brilliant piece of Romance? Where are the comrades we tented with on the Windy Plains? Many of

Christmas Eve, 1918. Taken in mid-ocean on board the Hospital Ship Essequibo—running between England and Canada. Frank Walker stands in the back row, third from left.

them have found their graves in France and Flanders, many are in hospitals, maimed or dying. Some few are well enough, left, as I am left; but we seem to have grown old before our time, and we do not enjoy the companionship, even of ourselves.

"All, all are gone, the old familiar faces!"

During the Fall of 1918, I was transferred from the Medical Corps Depot, at Shorncliffe, to the staff of the Hospital Ship *Neuralia* running between England and Canada. On this ship, and on the *Essequibo* I made, altogether, eight return trips, and at the expiration of this time (the war having then come to a close) was allowed to return Home.[7]

F. Walker

---

7. Sir Andrew Macphail's *The Medical Services*, XIX, p. 239, states that in the work of evacuating the sick and wounded to Canada, the service employed five hospital ships, which made an aggregate of 42 voyages. The *Essequibo* made 20 voyages transporting 5,106 patients, and the *Neuralia* made three voyages transporting 1,950 patients.

Frank Walker, April, 1954.

Epilogue

Mary F. Gaudet

With the Great War behind him but never far from his consciousness, Pte. Frank Walker received his discharge from the Army Medical Corps in Halifax, in July 1919, eight months after the War had come to a close. Finally, he was able to come home to his beloved mother in Charlottetown and begin to reshape a life forever changed by war. Determined to be a reporter, he enrolled in a Charlottetown business school shortly after his return, in order to gain the necessary skills that would launch him into a career in journalism. It was a profession he would serve faithfully for over half a century.

It is my understanding that my father began his career as a recorder with the Charlottetown Courthouse, from where he was hired a couple of years later by J. R. Burnett, publisher of an afternoon newspaper, *The Charlottetown Examiner*. When Mr. Burnett acquired part ownership of *The Charlottetown Guardian*, a morning daily, he invited "Mr. Walker" to join his newsroom staff. Under the kind and fatherly guidance of the Scottish-born Burnett, Dad learned the ropes as a cub reporter. Over the years, he continued to hone his journalistic skills as he covered the various newsroom assignments, along with the Prince Edward Island Legislature and the Charlottetown Courthouse. His coverage of the proceedings of the provincial Legislature was so painstakingly accurate that it earned him the title "Mr. Hansard." There was no official record of legislative debates, noted political scientist Dr. Frank MacKinnon in 1951, but "It is the general opinion among Island public men, Liberal and Conservative, that Mr. Walker's reports are accurate, fair and reliable accounts of the proceedings, and they are frequently referred to as an unofficial Hansard on the floor of the House itself."

During the last thirty-five years or so of his career, my father served as the associate editor of *The Charlottetown Guardian*. His accuracy as a reporter was now matched by the force of his opinions. As his obituary would observe, "Strong in his convictions Mr. Walker was a staunch supporter of Island rights under Confederation and politicians of all stripes had been the target of his pointed sarcasm and biting wit." At the same time, as one admiring reader remembered, his editorials "were always in good taste and never stooping to meanness."

131 ❧ *Journal and Poems of Pte. Frank Walker*

For a number of years, it was my father's practice to collect historical tidbits pertinent to Prince Edward Island from various printed sources. He published them regularly under the heading "Old Charlottetown," with each item chosen to correspond with the current date or a current issue. At a time when there was little Island history being written or published, this feature was very popular, and it is still remembered. It was very much a reflection of Dad's love of history and literature.[1] "On Island history and politics," Hillsborough MP Heath Macquarrie would comment after Dad's death, "Frank Walker stands supreme."

As editor, there were few social or political injustices that escaped my father's watchful eye. I particularly remember an incident during the 1940s. An internationally renowned orchestra was booked to perform in Charlottetown, and made reservations at the Charlottetown Hotel. Upon arrival, the musicians were refused accommodation because they were black. The city's other major hotel, the Queen, graciously welcomed them. Such incidents provided material for my father's biting editorials, which often reflected his personal outrage.

Other incidents affected Dad more personally. In 1941, the Island justice system passed its last sentence of death. Two young men were convicted of the brutal murder of an elderly storekeeper. My father was invited, as press representative, to witness the execution. The prisoners were hanged back to back. One man did not die immediately, and the executioner had to intervene. For my father, who had seen so much of death during the War, this particular instance of retributive justice was equally unsettling, and it remained with him for a long time.

The most profound change during my father's editorial tenure came in December 1953, when *The Charlottetown Guardian* came under new ownership and management. My father moved reluctantly from the warm family atmosphere cultivated by Mr. Burnett and his sons into the corporate administration of the Thomson media conglomerate. It would be less than accurate to say that Dad adapted cheerfully to the new order. While the institution of a cost-shared pension plan proved beneficial to him in his later years, he had grave concerns about the increasing trend in the industry toward commercialism; he felt that the independence and integrity of the newspaper would be compromised.

---

1.   The Public Archives and Records Office in Charlottetown houses a number of "Old Charlottetown" columns, thanks to Bill Burnett, a friend and former co-worker of my father.

Despite his apprehensions, my father continued to follow his calling. When ill health finally forced his retirement in 1969, two months short of his seventy-sixth birthday, *The Guardian* noted that a journalistic era, marked by one man's dedication to accuracy and objectivity, had ended.

In 1923, when Dad was thirty years old, single, and living with his mother, he met Margaret Aurelie Weir, a stenographer at *The Charlottetown Guardian* office. Although she was ten years his junior, the attraction was mutual, and the relationship grew into love. In 1925, the year following his mother's death, my father and mother were married in Charlottetown at the Bishop's Palace, as was the custom in that day for a marriage between a Roman Catholic and a person of a different denomination. (Mom was a Catholic, Dad a Presbyterian.) From their union, seven children were born: Margaret Corinne, Mary Florence, John Masefield, Mildred Bennett, George Meredith, Priscilla Jean, and Elizabeth Anne. My father's life at home was extremely routine, considering the hustle and bustle of his large family; he depended entirely on my mother to juggle the schedules of seven children around those of church, home, and school.

As a child, there was no doubt in my mind that my Dad was a workaholic. He worked regular hours during the day and for a couple of hours most evenings. He never took holidays when we were young, but, in the 1940s, he suffered the first of several heart attacks, which forced him to slow down a little. On Saturday and Sunday afternoons, he relaxed with his books and music, often sharing them with a former school chum and World War I veteran, Fred Taylor. We children grew up surrounded by a home library of literature's finest works and an equally fine collection of classical music.

Despite the long hours Dad devoted to his work, he often shared his love of poetry with us. He was especially fond of the 18th-century poet Robert Burns. This was not surprising, given Dad's Scottish heritage. Nor was it accidental that we children delighted in his recitations of the immortal "Tam O'Shanter" and "To A Mouse." The "Bard of Scotland" remained one of his favourite poets, in whom he took great delight. Sometimes he would talk about the War and his comrades, for whom he had the greatest respect. Frequently, he would recite his own poem, "Packing Out: A Ballad of the Stretcher Bearers." This became a family favourite.

Dad also shared his love of music with us. When I was small, he would sit me on his knee while he listened to recordings of symphonic music. He would take my hand in his, and with an imaginary baton we would conduct the orchestra.

The formal address "Mr. Walker," as Dad was generally known, accurately conveyed the respect, the very private person, the old-school gentleman, and the student/scholar persona that emanated from my father in both his public and private life. Underneath this serious exterior, however, there was a lively sense of humour which, on occasion, served us children well. My father's secret to a contemplative Saturday afternoon was to ensure that we received our weekly allowance. Every Saturday, when he arrived home from the office at noon, we would be waiting, not so patiently, for the treats that he always brought—and for our weekly allowance. Initially, this stipend was sufficient to cover a matinee at the Capitol Theatre and a bag of penny candy. After some years, as the price of admission increased and inflation cut into our weekly candy purchases, we felt that it was appropriate to alert Dad to our financial hardship. A couple of us, in a very serious address, informed him that "we raised you." The raise was immediately forthcoming, and it was to be adjusted many times during our adolescence. Many years later, Dad cheerfully reminded me of the day that we had "raised him."

The year following Dad's retirement from *The Guardian*, we celebrated our parents' forty-fifth wedding anniversary. Two years later, my mother suffered a series of progressive strokes, and was confined to a nursing home for a short time, until her death on 23 May 1973, at the age of seventy-one. Over the next few years, Dad's health seriously deteriorated. He entered the same private nursing home, where he died on 24 November 1977, one month short of his eighty-fourth birthday.

Many Islanders remember "Mr. Walker of *The Guardian*" for his spirited editorials, his "Old Charlottetown" column, his fearless public advocacy, and his gentlemanly mien. Some Islanders remember my father's literary pursuits, including the study of Latin in his mid-fifties in order to read Dante and other authors in their original language. A few of us remember the very private, contemplative man whose material needs were minimal, but who always provided generously for his family.

There are no World War I comrades left to remember Pte. Frank Walker, the stretcher bearer with the bent for poetry, the war-weary veteran who, in 1918, asked, "Where are the merry, care-free crew –? / Where are the comrades we tented with on the Windy Plains?" My father's War Journal and poetry are a testimony to those who found their graves in France or Flanders, "leaving a song unsung, a tale untold," and to those who returned home "old before their time." They, like my father, had to reshape their lives to accommodate the horrors of a war that would be forever a significant part of their memory bank.

From a Stretcher-Handle allows us to journey with the foot soldiers of the Great War from their youthful, exuberant march forward to "Glory and Adventure" to the stark realization that war really has no glory. My father's personal account gives an emotional depth to our understanding of World War I that statistics and overviews cannot convey. His words poignantly serve as a clarion call to remembrance for our generation and for generations to come.

Bibliography
"You Have No Idea..." Stretcher Bearers in the Great War
by Boyde Beck

Block, Ernest G. *I Want One Volunteer*. Toronto: Ryerson Press, 1965.

Boyd, William. *With a Field Ambulance at Ypres*. Toronto: Musson Books Co., 1916.

Duguid, Col. A. Fortesque. *Official History of the Canadian Forces in the Great War, 1914–1919*. Ottawa: King's Printer, 1938.

Ellis, John. *Eye-Deep in Hell: Trench Warfare in World War I*. New York: Pantheon Books, 1976.

——. *The Sharp End: The Fighting Man in World War II*. New York: Charles Scribner's Sons, 1980.

Essame, H. *The Battle for Europe, 1918*. New York: Charles Scribner's Sons, 1972.

Fussell, Paul. *The Great War and Modern Memory*. London: Oxford University Press, 1975.

Keirstead, Robin Glen. "The Canadian Military Medical Experience During the Great War, 1914–1918." Unpublished MA Thesis. Kingston: Queen's University, 1982.

Macphail, Sir Andrew. *Official History of the Canadian Forces in the Great War, 1914–1919: The Medical Services*. Ottawa: King's Printer, 1925.

Nasmith, Col. George A. *Canada's Sons and Great Britain in the World War*. Toronto: Thomas Allen, 1919.

Noyes, Frederick W. *Stretcher Bearers... At the Double!* Toronto: Hunter, Rose, 1937.

Pottle, Frederick A. *Stretchers: The Story of a Hospital Unit on the Western Front*. New Haven: Yale University Press, 1929.

Rawling, Bill. *Surviving Trench Warfare: Technology and the Canadian Corps, 1914–1918*. Toronto: University of Toronto Press, 1991.

Roland, Charles G. "Battlefield Surgery and the Stretcher-bearers' Experience." *Norman Bethune: his times and his legacy*, Shephard, David and Andrée Lévesque, eds. The Canadian Public Health Association, 1982.

Winter, Denis. *Death's Men: Soldiers of the Great War*. London: Penguin Books, 1978.

Bibliography
Introduction and Epilogue
by Mary F. Gaudet

Primary Sources

Beatty, David Pierce. *Memories Of The Forgotten War: The World War I Diary Of Pte. V. E. Goodwin.* Port Elgin, New Brunswick: Baie Verte Editions, 1986.

———. *The Vimy Pilgrimage, July, 1936: From The Diary of Florence Murdock.* Amherst, N.S.: Acadian Printing, 1987.

Christie, Norm. *For King & Empire.* Winnipeg: Bunker to Bunker Books: 1996.

Dole, Nathan Haskell. *Robert Burns's Complete Poetical Works.* New York: Thomas Y. Crowell Company, 1900.

Giesler, Patricia. *Valour Remembered: Canada and the First World War.* Ottawa: Minister of Veterans Affairs, 1982.

Hammond's Family Reference World Atlas. New revised ed. Garden City, New York: Hanover House.

Ingoldsby, Thomas. *The Ingoldsby Legends, or Mirth and Marvels.* 6th ed. London: J. M. Dent & Sons, Ltd., 1930.

Lord, Walter, ed. *The Freemantle Diary.* New York: Capricorn Books, 1960.

Macphail, Sir Andrew. *Official History Of The Canadian Forces In The Great War 1914–1919: The Medical Services.* Ottawa: Minister of National Defence. 1925.

Michelin Road Atlas of France. New York: Crown Publishers, Inc.

Secondary Sources

Morrison, J. Clinton, Jr. *Hell Upon Earth: A Personal Account of Prince Edward Island Soldiers in the Great War, 1914–1918.* Summerside, P.E.I.: 1989.

Still, William N. Jr. ed. *The Queenstown Patrol, 1917: The Diary of Commander Joseph K. Taussig, U.S. Navy.* Rhode Island: Naval War College Press, 1996.

Wheeler, Victor W. *No Man's Land: The 50th Battalion.* Alberta: Historical Resources Foundation, 1980.

National Archives

Canadian Expeditionary Forces Sailing Lists: Nos. 1, 2, 3, Feild Ambulances: Nominal Roll of Officers, Non-Commissioned Officers and Men. Courtesy of Donna Porter, Directorate of History and Heritage, Department of National Defence, Ottawa.

Lloyd's Registor of Shipping 1914–1918. Courtesy of Donna Porter, Directorate of History and Heritage, Department of National Defence, Ottawa.

The Access to Information and Privacy Section, Personnel Record Section. Client Services and Communication Branch, Ottawa.

INDEX

T

tanks, 103.
training, 23, 27, 35, 37, 39.
treatment of wounded, x, xii, xiii.
trenches, xiii, xiv, xv, 57, 59, 65, 69,
  83, 85, 87, 89, 93, 99, 101, 107,
  121.

U

uniforms, 27.

V

Valcartier Camp, 25.
Vimy Ridge, Battle of, 117, 119, 121.
Vimy, xvii.
Vlamertinghe, 67, 91, 93.

W

Walker, George, xvi, xvii.
Walker, Frank, **22, 26, 38, 76, 128,
  130.**
Walker, Christina, xvi, xvii, **22, 24.**
Watou, 65, 69.
Western Front, x, xviii.
Willerval, 123, 125.
wounded, xii, xiii, 57, 59, 67, 69,
  85, 93, 109, 119, 125.
wounds, xi, xii, 39.
Wulverghem, 83.

Y

Ypres, xvii, 65, 67, 69, 71, 87, 88,
  90, 91, 95.
  Battle of, 87.
Ypres Salient, 69, 86, 93.